MUSLIM SEPARATISM
Causes and Consequences

SITA RAM GOEL

VOICE OF INDIA
New Delhi

First Published 1985
Fifth Reprint 1987
Second Revised and Enlarged Reprint 1995
Reprint 2019, 2020

ISBN 978-81-85990-26-2

Website: www.voiceofin.com

Published by Voice of India, 2/18, Ansari Road, New Delhi – 110 002.
Printed at Replika Press Pvt. Ltd.

MUSLIM SEPARATISM
CAUSES AND CONSEQUENCES

CONTENTS

CHAPTER I
THE TWO BEHAVIOUR PATTERNS

"Pakistan and Bangladesh are their fixed deposits. Those are Islamic states. No one else can lay a claim on them. India is a joint account. Plunder it as much as you please."[1] This is how Shri Shiva Prasad Roy, a very perceptive Bengali writer, has summed up the present situation in what is described as the Indian subcontinent now a days but what has been known as Bharatavarsha since time immemorial.

Shri Roy could have easily extended the logic and concluded that Afghanistan was another fixed deposit created by the Muslims quite some time before Pakistan and Bangladesh came into existence. Afghanistan, too, has been an Islamic state since its inception. But Shri Roy is not the only Hindu to have missed that point. Hindu society as a whole has ceased to remember that Afghanistan rose on the ruins of Gandhara and Kamboja, the two ancient *Janapadas* of Bharatavarsha which had stood guard on our North-Western gateway for ages untold.

Nor would Hindu society like to remember that Baluchistan, North-West Frontier Province, Sindh, West Punjab, East Bengal and Sylhet were constituent units of the motherland a mere 40 years ago. Hindu society would feign forget the Partition in 1947 if the Islamic crusaders inside the residue that is Hindustan did not continue to remind it that Partition was by no means a closed chapter. A proof positive of its own preference in the matter is provided by a plethora of studies on the subject published in this country in the years following 1947.

STALE STUDIES OF PARTITION

All these studies describe in varying details the British game of divide-and-rule; the growth of Muslim fears of 'Hindu domination' after the Indian National Congress was founded in 1885; the rise of the Muslim League as a reaction to 'Hindu revivalism' in the wake of the Swadeshi Movement; the sabotage of efforts at Hindu-Muslim settlement by the grant of separate electorates under the Minto-Morley Reforms; the short-lived communal amity after the Lucknow Pact (1916) and during the Khilafat agitation (1920-22) under the leadership of Mahatma Gandhi and the Ali Brothers; the failure of fresh efforts for a Hindu-Muslim settlement under the initiative from C.R. Das and

---

[1] Shiv Prasad Roy, *Dibbagyen Noy, Kāṇḍagyen Chai,* Calcutta, 1982.

Motilal Nehru; the mistake made by the Congress when it refused to accommodate the Muslim League in provincial ministries formed in 1937; the 'resultant' rise of Muslim separatism culminating in the Lahore Resolution of the League in 1940; the failure of the Cripps Mission due to last minute machinations of Churchill; the move made by Wavell to break the deadlock in 1945 on the basis of the Desai-Liaqat agreement; the 'torpedoing' of the Cabinet Mission Plan by an 'ill-advised' statement of Pandit Nehru; the Direct Action launched by the Muslim League in August 1946 and the large-scale communal riots; the 'disillusionment' of Sardar Patel due to his 'bitter experience' of the Congress-League coalition; the award of the Radcliff Boundary Commission and the consequent blood-bath on both sides of the borders; and the final drop of the curtain on a dismal drama when the 'Father of the Nation' was martyred by a 'Hindu fanatic'. The one unmistakable impression which these studies leave on a reader's mind is that the whole bloody business is by now a part of the dead past and should excite no one except those who specialize in archival excavations. It is regarded as a serious violation of scholarship to see some pattern, psychological or ideological, in these developments.

Of course, the politicians who parade themselves as guardians of Secularism — a doctrine proclaimed after Partition—are not prepared to leave it at that. They tell us, in very grave tones, that the tragedy that took place on the eve of independence has a lesson to teach to the nation. They seem to be convinced that it was 'Hindu communalism' which divided the country and killed the 'greatest Indian born after Gautama Buddha'. And they warn us that 'Hindu communalism' which was lying low for a few years is again striving to stage a comeback in order to subvert the secular 'struggle for national integration'. They are never tired of talking about a 'Hindu backlash'.[2]

Some of these secularist politicians swear by Mahatma Gandhi and his *sarva-dharma-samabhāva.* Many more swear by Socialism which gives a good opportunity to the Communists and fellow-travellers to steal the whole show for their own ends. One can also spot, in these secularist ranks, many Mullahs playing the old separatist game under the cover of new slogans. But there are hardly any politicians who dare question the character or claims of this Secularism which has attained the status of a national consensus. The only jarring note is heard when the self-appointed high-priests of Secularism stigmatise some political and socio-cultural organisations as communal, and when the spokes-

[2] The latest phrase patronised by Secularism is 'Hindu fundamentalism'.

men of these 'guilty parties' bewail that they are being wrongly blamed and spend almost all their time in trying to prove their credentials to the contrary.

A BREATH OF FRESH BREEZE

It is in this stale atmosphere of sterile scholarship and sloganized politics that the book by Shri H.V. Seshadri has come like a breath of fresh breeze. *The Tragic Story of Partition*[3] is not only the latest but also the best study of this subject made so far. It gives us all the facts included in the earlier studies. It also takes into account many known but neglected facts. But what distinguishes it from all other studies, is its deeper probe and wider perspective in the interpretation of all facts and episodes.

This remarkable book has many facets, rich in ideological implications of a far-reaching import. We will take up those facets one by one in the chapters that follow. To start with, we want to take up what we consider to be its most important contribution, namely, the unravelling of two behaviour patterns — Muslim and National—which collaborated closely for years and precipitated Partition in the final round. The Muslim behaviour pattern was characterized by acrimony, accusations, complaints, demands, denunciations, and street riots. The National behaviour pattern, on the other hand, was characterized by acquiescence, assent, cajolery, concessions, cowardice, self-reproach, and surrender.

The two behaviour patterns have remained intact and are still operative. That is why the Partition in 1947 cannot and should not be considered a closed chapter. Moreover, the two behaviour patterns provide the key not only to a correct understanding of the complexities of present-day politics in India, but also to an anticipation of political developments in days to come.

THE MUSLIM BEHAVIOUR PATTERN

There is plenty of evidence to show that the Muslim behaviour pattern has remained true to type in the years after 1947. We have witnessed an increasing incidence of street riots staged by the same sort of Muslim hooligans, on the same sort of petty pretexts as in the years preceding Partition. Muslim spokesmen, no matter what political platform they use, have levelled the same sort of accusations, namely, that the Muslims are a 'poor and persecuted minority' entirely at mercy of a

---

[3] H.V. Seshadri, *The Tragic Story of Partition*, Bangalore, 1982.

'brute Hindu majority'; that 'Muslim lives, properties and honour' are not safe in the midst of a rising tide of 'Hindu communalism'; and that 'Hindu chauvinism' is seeking to wipe out all vestiges of Muslim religion and culture. It is the Pirpur Report[4] of the Muslim League, all over again.

Next comes the constant complaint that the Muslim community has had hardly any share in the national cake, particularly in the fruits of economic development that has taken place in the years after independence. We are told that Hindu business houses do not give jobs to deserving Muslims, that Hindu bureaucrats discriminate against Muslims in public sector undertakings and state-sponsored welfare projects, and that Hindu-dominated educational institutions deny every opportunity to the Muslims to improve their qualifications. We are also informed that Hindu vested interests conspire with Hindu hooligans, Hindu police and Hindu militiamen to destroy Muslim properties and wreck Muslim business establishments wherever and whenever the Muslims start getting prosperous by their 'own unaided enterprise'.[5]

These accusations and complaints have been followed by concrete demands which also remind us of pre-Partition days. The general demand is that Muslims should have not only reservations, proportionate to their population, but also weightages in all sectors and at all levels of national life, particularly the national administration including the armed forces. A few years ago, a Muslim spokesman[6] had demanded that 20 percent seats in the Parliament and the State Assemblies should be reserved for members of his community. He also recommended that the remaining 80 percent seats should be filled only by those persons whose selection before elections had been cleared by the same community!

Finally, Muslim spokesmen have threatened that if their complaints are not heeded and their demands not met, 'the Muslim masses will be forced to launch a struggle for securing justice for themselves'. Syed Shahabuddin, a luminary of the Janata Party, 'shudders to think of the day when Muslim young men lose patience and take to the streets'.[7] At the same time, they have invited all other 'minorities' to join them

---

[4] A report published by the Muslim League in 1938 listing 'atrocities committed against the Muslims' by the Congress Ministries since 1937. It has been reprinted recently from New Delhi.

[5] The noted journalist Kuldip Nayar swallowed this Muslim thesis and tried his best to popularise it after the Moradabad Riots. Many other Hindu-baiters have been retailing it with airs of profound scholarship.

[6] Imam Abdullah Bukhari of Jama Masjid, Delhi.

[7] He is now in the Janata Dal.

in a 'just struggle' for their rights. The 'other minorities' comprise not only the Christians but also Sikhs and so-called Adivasis and Harijans. One should not be surprised if the Jains and the Buddhists, the Jats and the Yadavas, the Vaishnavites and the Lingayats also receive similar invitations in the near future. After all, what is Hindu society but a 'medley of minorities', each with its own 'grievances'?

As this Muslim behaviour pattern unfolds further, a demand for separate electorates is bound to be the next logical as well as psychological step. The 'downtrodden Muslim masses' will 'discover' before long that they cannot expect a 'vigorous vocalization of their grievances' from representatives elected by a 'mixed population', even when some of these representatives happen to come from their own midst. In due course, pressure will be mounted for constituting Muslim majority districts, divisions and regions wherever the Muslims have a sizable population. These Muslim majority areas will clamour for becoming autonomous units like the Kashmir Valley so that 'the Muslims can decide their own destiny'. And these autonomous units will wait for an opportune time to federate with Pakistan or Bangladesh under the protection of this or that world-power, depending upon the configuration of world forces at that time. Meanwhile, Muslim majorities can be manipulated in many more districts by mass conversion of the weaker sections of Hindu society with the help of petro-dollars, by mass infiltration from Bangladesh and Pakistan, and by mass breeding in pursuance of 'divine' commands conveyed in the Quran and the Hadis. The contours of the campaign can be seen by all those who have not become blinded by secularist slogans, or have not been denationalized by a vote-hungry politics.

THE NATIONAL BEHAVIOUR PATTERN

There is also plenty of evidence to show that the National behaviour pattern vis-a-vis the Muslim 'minority' has also remained true to type in the years after independence. The National leadership is once again responding to this sinister situation in the same sloganized manner as had been stereotyped by its predecessors in the years preceding Partition. This leadership has once again failed to see the long-term strategy at the back of short-term tactics. The scene is once again being dominated by politicians who live from hand to mouth, who cannot see beyond their nose, who run a rat race for winning applause from the Muslims, whose eyes are galvanized greedily on the Muslim vote-bank, and who take the Hindu society for granted.

There are several straws in the wind that is blowing in different parts of the country. Urdu is being recognized as an official language in state after state even though Urdu teachers in schools and colleges have to sit idle for want of students. Academies are being set up in many state capitals in the name of Iqbal, an ardent advocate of Islamic imperialism. Kerala has given a lead in carving out Muslim majority districts, leaving the local Hindu population at the mercy of Mullahs and Muslim hooligans. Bengal under anti-national Communists and U.P. under a crumbling Congress edifice are most likely to walk into this Islamic trap before long. Several enquiry commissions or their reports have been suppressed because the verdict was likely to go or had gone against the Muslims in fixing the responsibility for riots. Jagannath Mishra of Bihar set the record in this race for *suppressio veri suggestio falsi* when he cooked up a summary of the Jamshedpur riots report in direct contradiction to the conclusions reached by the enquiry commission concerned, and palmed it off on the Parliamentarians and the Press.

Assam is the most poignant pointer to the way towards which things are heading. In the past, the Islamic imperialists who invaded India had to equip and bring along their own armies. But in the case of Assam, the same invader has been assured by the Government of India that he need not bother to bring along his own battalions and that all ammunition and manpower he needs will be supplied to him in India itself, free of cost and in ample measure. It is a different story that the patriots in Assam have fought back fiercely, though with bare hands, to meet and, many a time, repel the rapacious marauder. The Government of India on its part has left no stone unturned to aid and abet the aggressor.

NO WARNING VOICES

In the years preceding Partition, we had Sri Aurobindo, Swami Shraddhananda, Lala Lajpat Rai, Bipin Chandra Pal, Sarat Chandra Chatterjee, Veer Savarkar and Dr. Hedgewar who had studied and seen through Islam and who had sounded an alarm. Even Rabindra Nath Tagore had expressed his misgivings after exchanging notes with some Mullahs and Muslims politicians. It is a different matter that their voices had been drowned by the sermons which Mahatma Gandhi poured out in praise of the 'noble faith of Islam'. What remains significant in that old story is that these thinkers and writers had done their duty by their people. We hardly hear such voices of sanity in our present-day predicament. What we have, instead, is a large number of self-righteous or self-seeking politicians, hand-in-glove with scholars and scribes who have never done their homework in Islamic theology or Islamic history or Islamic theory of the state, and whose stock-in-trade is finding faults with a prostrate Hindu society.

The Tragic Story of Partition by Shri H.V. Seshadri, therefore, is a very welcome publication. It could not have come at a more opportune moment.

CHAPTER II
THE NATIONAL TERRITORIAL TRADITION

The perspective of *The Tragic Story of Partition* by Shri H.V. Seshadri is set by what the learned author has written in his short but succinct Preface. He says: "In the [past] one thousand years many parts of our country had been ruled by the Muslims and then by the British, but the nation had never compromised, in principle, its sovereignty over any part of the motherland. As a result, our nation had never ceased to strive for throwing out the aggressors and liberate those parts. And history tells us that ultimately it did succeed in freeing the entire land from the clutches of foreign invaders. However, for the first time, Partition conceded the moral and legal right to them over certain parts of the country and declared an ignominious finale to the one thousand years old heroic struggle for freedom. Thus it was an act of humiliating surrender on the point of principle. The usual interpretation of Partition, however, does not utter a word about this aspect. Even while conceding Partition to be a tragedy, it is sought to be made out as the only practical way out then available — as the inevitable price for achieving freedom."[1]

This is a very significant statement. Firstly, it carries within it a consciousness of the territorial and historical traditions cherished by the people of Bharatavarsha since ages past. Secondly, it brings out the point that the surrender of a national principle by a people is more suicidal than the surrender of national territory under unfavourable circumstances.

We shall take up the territorial tradition first. The vision of Bharatavarsha which had inspired our struggle against British imperialism has been described by Shri Seshadri in the very first chapter in the following words: "Indeed how many were the seers and sages, poets and prophets — right from the Vedic age upto the modern times — who had fostered in the nation's breast the integrated and whole picture of Bharat as the Divine Mother. Bharat, in their eyes, was not a mere clod of clay. It was verily the *Matrubhoomi*, the *Punyabhoomi*, the *Dharmabhoomi*, the *Devabhoomi*, the *Karmabhoomi* — all sublimated into one single majestic figure of Bharat Mata. To Bankimchandra, She appeared as the triple manifestation of Saraswati, Lakshmi and Durga. Rabindranath Tagore visualised Her as *Devi bhuvana-mana-mohini* — the divine enchantress of the world. To Swami Vivekananda, She was

[1] *The Tragic Story of Partition*, p. 12.

the Mother of all the thirty-three crores of gods and goddesses — whose worship would gratify all those myriad deities. Guruji Golwalkar visualised Her as Trinity of *Mata* — the loving mother, *Pita* — the protecting father, and *Guru* — the elevating spiritual guide. The unity of Bharat is so basic to its nature, so sublime in its depths — in fact, an inseparable aspect of its national soul."[2]

BHARATAVARSHA BECOMES A "MULTITUDE OF DIFFERENT COUNTRIES"

Shri Seshadri goes on to point out in the second chapter, Breaking the Hindu Morale, how Bharatavarsha "was newly painted by the British as a 'continent' or 'sub-continent', and not as a single country". He cites John Strachey who had "held some of the highest offices in India". In a series of lectures delivered in 1885 at the University of Cambridge, Strachey had said, "What is India? What does this name India really signify? The answer that I have sometimes given sounds paradoxical, but it is true. There is no such country and this is the first and most essential fact about India that can be learned. India is a name which we give to a great region including a multitude of different countries."[3] This great falsehood about our country was foisted upon generation after generation of Hindus by the British system of education till it passed into day-to-day political parlance. Rare is the scholar or politician who does not now refer to his country as the Indian or Indo-Pak subcontinent.

The very sound of 'Indian sub-continent' is shocking to the ears of those who have had the privilege of performing or participating in some Hindu *saṁskāras*. The wording of every *saṁkalpa,* starting with *Jambudvīpe Bharatakhaṇḍe,* invokes the opposite vision of a single, though vast and variegated land, inhabited by a people who are proud of being born and having lived in it. The territorial unity and integrity of Bharatavarsha — the land that lies south of the Himalayas, east of Sakadvipa (Seistan), south-east of Vāhlīka (Balkh), west of Burma and between the two seas — was never a political contrivance created by the sword of a conqueror. On the contrary, it was meant and manifested by Mother Nature herself as the cradle of an incomparable culture — the culture of *Sanātana Dharma.*

CULTURAL UNITY VERSUS POLITICAL UNITY

It is pointed out by superficial students of Indian history that the

---

[2] Ibid., p. 9.
[3] Ibid., p.12.

'Indian sub-continent' has been more often a congeries of independent and warring states than a single and sovereign political entity. But if they look a little deeper, they will soon discover a type of unity which far surpasses mere political unity and which has proved more permanent. This is the cultural unity of Bharatavarsha. The seers and sages of India have always placed political unity at the lowest rung of the ladder. What they have prized above all is a more abiding unity based on the very sound principles of *svabhāva, svadharma* and *svarājya,* nurtured by numerous regions and communities within a common framework of spiritual and moral values. To their perceptive eyes, political empires are passing phenomena which leave behind them nothing better than memories of bloodshed, coercion, and exploitation. Ashoka's imperialist adventure into Kalinga and the anguish and remorse it entailed in a sensitive soul has all along been cited as a classical example in this context.

Where is the empire of ancient Iran to-day, or that of Alexander of Macedonia, or that of ancient Rome, or that of the medieval Arabs? The empires built by the Turks, the Spaniards, the Portuguese, the Dutch, the British, the Belgians, and the French were far-flung fabrics till our own times. Did these empires create or leave behind them any sense of unity among the lands or the peoples over which they presided for long? On the other hand, the cultural unity that was envisaged by *Sanātana Dharma,* and embodied in tried and tested traditions in its laboratory of Bharatavarsha, is still a living force. In the final analysis, this cultural unity is the only guarantee of a political unity in the face of so many fissiparous forces let loose by self-alienated scholars and secularist politicians.

The Mahabharata carries a complete picture of this cultural unity in its *tīrtha-yātrā-parva*, which is part of the larger *Vana-parva.* The Pandavas accompany their *Purohita,* Dhaumya, on a long pilgrimage to all parts of Bharatavarsha. They pay their homage to many mountains, rivers, *saṁgamas,* lakes, tanks, forest groves and other sacred shrines which had become hallowed by association with Gods and Goddesses, *rishis* and *munis, satees* and *sādhvees,* heroes and heroines. And they feel fulfilled as they never did before or after in their long lives. The same Pandavas made an imperial conquest of the whole country, not once but twice and performed a *rājasūya yajña* at the end of each triumph. But the Pandava empire is a faint memory of the forgotten past. On the other hand, the sacred spots which the Pandavas visited during their one and only pilgrimage, draw millions of devotees in our own days as they did in the distant past, long before the Pandvas appeared on the scene.

The politicians have bartered away several precious parts of the motherland and betrayed the people who had lived in those parts for untold ages. The same brood is now busy beating up provincial passions on every petty pretext. But the common people still flock to all ancient pilgrimage places in the residue that is Hindustan. The common people still pay the homage of their hearts to those sacred shrines also which have been left in hostile hands, whenever they listen to recitations of the Bhagavata and the Mahabharata. Even the national anthem adopted by those who surrendered to Islamic imperialism, pays homage to Panjāba, Sindha and Banga which are now supposed to be foreign lands. Rabindranath who composed and sang this great song had the whole of Bharatavarsha imprinted on his mind and heart. He had never heard of the 'Indian sub-continent'.

The Ramayana, the Puranas and the Dharmashastras paint the same portrait of an ancient land, every spot of which is sacred to some cultural memory or the other. The Jainagama and the Tripitaka speak again and again of sixteen Mahajanapadas which spanned the spread of Bharatavarsha in the life-time of Bhagvan Mahavira and the Buddha. Even a dry compendium on grammar, the Ashtadhyayi of Panini, provides a near complete count of all the Janapadas in ancient India—Gandhara and Kamboja, Sindhu and Sauvira, Kashmir and Kekaya, Madra and Trigarta, Kuru and Panchala, Kaushala and Kashi, Magadha and Videha, Anga and Vanga, Kirata and Kamarupa, Suhma and Udra, Vatsa and Matsya, Abhira and Avanti, Nishadha and Vidarbha, Dandakaranya and Andhra, Karnataka and Kerala, Chola and Pandya. The epic poetry poured out by Kalidasa, Magha, Bharavi and Sriharsha continues the same tradition of talking endlessly about Bharatavarsha as a single and indivisible geographical entity, as a *karmabhūmi* for Gods and Goddesses, Brahmarshis and Rajarshis, and as higher than heaven for all those who have had the good fortune of being born in it.

The names of places and provinces had changed considerably by the time the Buddhist pilgrims — Fa-hien, Hiuen-Tsang and It-sing — came to India in the 4th, 7th and 8th centuries. But the ancient contours of Bharatavarsha as a self-contained territorial unit had not undergone any change. The pilgrims from China found themselves on the sacred land which they had come to visit as soon as they stepped into what is now known as Afghanistan. Many other lands beyond this North-Western province of India worshipped the Buddha and were dotted with Buddhist temples and monasteries. But the Chinese pilgrims did not experience the same spiritual stir in those lands as they did on entering the holy land which had given birth to the Buddha.

The three Chinese travellers have left detailed accounts of stupas and temples, schools and colleges, Brahmins and Bhikshus, kings and courtiers, classes and masses, towns and villages, mores and manners, customs and traditions. These accounts also leave the same impression of a deep cultural unity in the midst of many apparent diversities. They testify to the fundamental fact that no inhabitant of Bhāratavarsha, no matter what province or region he came from and no matter what language or dialect he spoke, felt like a foreigner in any other province or region.

It was this feeling of being at home everywhere in the country which took the Adi Shankaracharya from the southernmost tip to the farthest corners of Bharatavarsha in North and East and West and helped him found (or revive) the four foremost *dhāmas* at Badrinath, Dvaraka, Rameshvaram and Puri. There is no count of sadhus and sannyasins and house-holders who have travelled ever since on the trail blazed by that great acharya. Six and a half centuries later, Guru Nanak Dev followed in the footsteps of the Pandavas and the Shankaracharya in search of spiritual company. Chaitanyadeva who lived in the 16th century and Swami Vivekananda who came towards the end of the 19th, roamed over the same route, feeling similarly at home everywhere.

THE CHARACTER OF POLITICAL UNITY

It is not that the authors of this deeper and firmer unity had no conception of political unity. Only they did not give primacy to political unity, nor promote it at the cost of cultural unity. That was why they did not sanction the destruction or eclipse of local dynasties, or the socio-political autonomies of various regions and provinces, or the local cultural traditions, by any empire-builder. Nor did they sanction imperialist adventures outside the bounds of Bharatavarsha for subjugating people who did not belong to the national family.

The image of the whole of Bharatavarsha being a *chakravartikshetra* is as old as the oldest Vedic literature. The Itihasa-Purana provide glorious accounts of many *chakravartins*—Ikshvaku, Puru, Prithu Vainya, Sivi Ausinara, Mandhata, Raghu and so on—who accompanied the *aśvamedha* horse demanding submission from all kingdoms and republics, big and small, spread all over the country. The *rājasūya yajña* which was performed at the end of this campaign was more in the nature of a meeting of equals than a durbar held by a despot in order to humble or humiliate subordinate princes and patriarchs. Sri

Krishna had demanded death for Jarasandha because the latter had violated this dharmic tradition of empire-building, and kept a hundred kings captive in his castle. The Nandas had won notoriety as an ignoble dynasty because they had also violated the standard code of conduct laid down by the *rājadharma* for righteous emperors, destroyed many local dynasties, and reduced other princes to provincial satraps.

And we have no record of an Indian empire-builder crossing over to foreign lands in search of conquests. Chandragupta Maurya (or Chandragupta I of the Gupta Dynasty according to an alternate chronology) could have easily overrun the Macedonian empire in West Asia after defeating Seleucus Nikator, But he stopped at the borders of Bharatavarsha after throwing out the foreign invader. So did Samudragupta after rounding off his victorious march in the Uttarapatha, however rich and inviting the lands beyond the borders might have been. This traditional taboo on going out and destroying the *dasyu* (aggressor) in the latter's own homeland was to prove quite costly in subsequent periods. It even degenerated into what is known as the Panipat mentality of waiting for the invader till he reached a particular field of battle. But what we wish to emphasize here is that there was a well-defined tradition of empire-building in India and thus providing political unity to the whole country.

DEFENCE OF THE NORTH-WESTERN FRONTIER

Before the British invader entered from the South and the East, it was the North-Western border of Bharatavarsha which was battered and breached again and again by a series of foreign invaders. That border, therefore, became an abiding part of national consciousness. This awareness is writ large in many a battle fought in defence of that border. Skandagupta had stormed towards that border in his fight to the finish against the Huna (or Saka) hordes. Later on, when Bharatavarsha was threatened by an Islamic invasion under the Arabs, some of the bravest battles were fought, and fought very successfully, in defence of Kabul and Zabul and Sindh. Still later, many Indian princes rallied round the Hindu Shahiya Dynasty of Udbhandapur, first in order to recover Kabul which had been overrun by the Islamicized Turks under Subuktigin, and then to contain the invasion by the same Turks after Indian forces had suffered a setback in the first endeavour.[4]

In more recent times, after the stranglehold of Islamic imperialism had been broken, the Marathas marched towards the same border im-

4. See Sita Ram Goel, *History of Heroic Hindu Resistance to Muslim Invaders* (636 A.D. to 1206 A.D.), Voice of India, 1984 reprinted in 1994.

pelled by the same national instinct and aspiration for freeing the motherland from all traces of foreign rule. The Sikhs under Maharaja Ranjit Singh fought some of their fiercest battles in the North-West to recover national territory from the Pathans who had meanwhile become alienated from the national mainstream after several centuries of subjugation to Islamic terror. The success achieved by the Marathas and the Sikhs was spectacular and was applauded by our people as a whole. On the other hand, the defeat of the Marathas in the Third Battle of Panipat was regarded as a national disaster and mourned far and wide. The Jats of Bharatpur who had plundered and harassed many imperial armies of the Mughals opened their doors as well as their purse-strings to provide succour and shelter to the worn-out Maratha veterans returning from Panipat.

Neither Chandragupta nor Samudragupta felt for a moment that he was intruding into foreign territory when he subdued the smaller principalities in the areas which have come to be known as Afghanistan and Pakistan in our own times. Nor did Skandagupta or Jayapala Shahiya or the Marathas or the Sikhs suffer from such an uncomfortable feeling when they set out to repel the Huna (or Saka) and Islamic invaders. Conversely, the Macedonian invader had proclaimed that he had entered India only after he had crossed what is now known as the Hindukush mountain. Greek historians leave no doubt that the army of Alexander which retreated by the land route through Baluchistan regarded itself as still inside India, and not free from the danger of Indian counter-attacks, till it had crossed over into the desert of Makran. The Arab chroniclers recorded again and again that the armies sent by successive Caliphs against Kabul and Zabul and Sindh had gone out for the conquest of Hind.

SURRENDER OF A VITAL PRINCIPLE

Shri Seshadri has, therefore, rightly pointed out that the national leadership surrendered a very vital principle and betrayed a very old and cherished territorial tradition when it conceded a permanent alienation of people and territory on both sides of the borders, and accepted the British definition of Bharatavarsha as a sub-continent constituted of many countries and communities. He observes with great anguish in his very first chapter, Crucial Hour of Freedom Struggle, that "Millions of devoted and loving children of Bharatavarsha had been overnight turned into subjects of a fanatically anti-Hindu State. River Sindhu became alien to crores of her progeny and the birth-place of the Vedas was turned over to their inveterate foes. Crores upon crores of brothers and sisters on either side of the dividing line became foreigners to each other. Lakhs perished in the ensuing genocide. Unspeakable atrocities were let loose on men, women and children. Temples, pilgrimage centres and all holy places were razed to the ground."[5]

It would have been one thing to concede Partition because it could not be prevented at that time due to a combination of powerful and hostile forces brought into play by the British game to divide-and-rule, by the parasitic Islamic imperialism, and by the failure of the national leadership to evolve an appropriate strategy for a total liberation of the motherland from every vestige of foreign rule. But it was quite another thing to concede that the lands grabbed by the rearguard action of a retreating Islamic imperialism had become foreign lands for ever, and that the people alienated and subjugated by an Islamic state had become foreign nationals till the end of time. The former concession could have been forgiven as a state of helplessness in a particular situation. The latter concession was, without doubt, a cowardly surrender by a leadership which had lost its moorings in the national tradition of India's territorial integrity.

This loss of the national territorial tradition was the direct result of a loss of proper vision pertaining to national history. Shri Seshadri refers to this latter loss also before he sets out on his main theme.

---

[5] *The Tragic Story of Partition*, p.10.

Chapter III
THE NATIONAL HISTORICAL TRADITION

The Partition of India which the national leadership conceded in principle in 1947 was a gross violation of the national territorial tradition which had always cherished the whole of Bharatavarsha as a single and indivisible Hindu homeland. But what was still more serious, it was also a flagrant betrayal of the national historical tradition which had never accepted the consolidation of any foreign conquest in any part of Bharatavarsha as a settle fact, final for all time.

Shri H.V. Seshadri has given, at the very start of *The Tragic Story of Partition,* an outline of the well-known national historical tradition — how the Hindus drove out the Macedonian marauders under Alexander after a short and swift struggle; how they first fought and defeated the Saka, Kushana and Huna hordes and finally absorbed these foreigners in the vast fabric of Hindu society and culture; how they resisted the Islamic invaders at every step for several centuries and then rolled back the barbarians by means of a multipronged counter-attack; and how they wrested freedom from British imperialism by a century-long struggle which was cultural or constitutional, revolutionary or non-violent according to the need of the hour.

It is in the context of this national historical tradition that he comments of Pandit Nehru's famous speech on the midnight of 15 August 1947. He asks in pain and anguish: "Did the 'tryst with destiny' which our leaders had made long years ago include this crucial twist of history also? Was it a picture of a divided Bharat which had been the cherished vision of our freedom fighters including Pandit Nehru?"

PARALYSIS AT THE TIME OF PARTITION

The first Prime Minister of an India, which had been partitioned by the residues of Islamic imperialism, was mighty pleased with himself as he picked up some pompous phrases from a foreign tongue and as a captive audience clapped. In his highly romanticized rhetoric, he had time only for a brief and grudging reference to the great tragedy that had engulfed millions of men and women and children in this country, at that very moment.

Mahatma Gandhi was meanwhile busy fighting the flames ignited by his own mistaken policies, and bemoaning the 'bad behaviour' of his own people whom he had sold to the butcher without a word of warning. He was soon to stake his life in order to finance the fiend whom he had tried his best to befriend all through his life but who had failed him at every step.

Sardar Patel was the only leader around who could survey the sorry scene with the eyes of a statesman, without wearing glasses borrowed from Soviet Russia, and without invoking the Gita and the Quran in the same breath. He picked up the pieces which had been left loose by an imperial order that was passing away, and welded them into a unity. But he was soon branded as a 'Hindu communalist' and an 'arch reactionary' by a motley crowd of traitors orchestrated from Moscow.

Another test came slightly later in Jammu and Kashmir which a Hindu prince had managed to save from the Islamic monster in spite of machinations by Mountbatten and British die-hards, and in the face of undisguised hostility from a Soviet stooge masquerading as the Prime Minister of India. But a large part of that precious patrimony was soon surrendered to Islamic imperialism in order to demonstrate India's 'democratic' credentials before an international opinion which wondered for quite some time why India was smitten with such a grave sense of guilt. The rest of the region, which had been saved by a brave soldiery at the cost of so much blood and toil, was handed over to a haughty sheikh who had never hidden his intention of setting up a separate sultanate. The Valley was very soon barred even to the sons of the soil who had to flee from their homes in the Pakistan-occupied parts of Jammu and Kashmir.

No one among the national leadership had the time or the talent to take stock of the situation, see the forces at work in a historical setting, and give a resounding call for a new national resolve — to foil the consolidation of Islamic imperialism in several parts of Bharatavarsha, and to launch another struggle for winning back all our people and every bit of national territory from the stranglehold of a theocratic state that was fast taking shape. The millions of Hindus who had to abandon their ancestral homes in East and West, became refugees at the very dawn of freedom for which they had worked so hard and made so many sacrifices. Their dream of becoming the proud citizens of a country freed from every vestige of foreign imperialism had suddenly turned into a nightmare. Something had gone seriously wrong somewhere.

DEGENERATION DUE TO DISTORTED VISION

Shri Seshadri traces this degeneration of the national vision to a distortion of our history by the British. He says: "Under Macaulay's dispensation our history opened with the chapter — 'The Dark Age' — which was, in fact, a period of Bharat's unparalleled achievements in material as well as spiritual fields. Then followed the periods — Hindu,

Muslim and British. The intent behind this kind of classification was obvious. The land belonged to those who for that period held the sceptre at Delhi. There were none who could he called the original children of this land, its natural masters. He who wielded the rod — to him the country belonged."[1]

This version of Indian history had serious ideological implications, Shri Seshadri has spelled them out as follows: "It was from now on that under the benign auspices of the British a new nation, a new people had to take shape out of the heterogeneous mass of human beings inhabiting here. That the expression 'a nation in the making' freely played on the lips of our English-educated proved with what utter devotion they were lapping up the new homilies."[2] The British masters wanted the 'natives' to feel grateful for giving to the latter a sense of history and a notion of nationhood.

The distortion cannot be dismissed as an injury inflicted in the past when the British presided over our education. The distortion is still being dished out by all our educational institutions and is being made progressively more pernicious. The government of an independent India is now concocting a still more mischievous version of Indian history and selling it on a large scale in the name of national integration.[3] No one seems to know that the old British version has been radically revised in recent years by the British scholars themselves.

It is true that Hindu society had never written its own history in the modern sense of the subject. It had never searched for archaeological and archival materials to knit together an account of monarchs and ministers or of military generals and civil administrators. We should be grateful to the British and other Western scholars for digging up our past and giving us a lead in writing our history in a modern and more ordered manner.

What we are pointing out is that the Western version of our history was not always objective. Quite often, this version was vitiated by cultural presuppositions and prejudices of which Western scholars had failed to purge themselves. In certain cases, this version was politically motivated as well.

THE NATIONAL VERSION OF INDIAN HISTORY

Hindu society had the Mahabharata, the Ramayana, the Puranas, the Prabandhas, the Mahakavyas, the Gathas, the Kathas, the Khyats

---

[1] Ibid., p.16.

[2] Ibid.

[3] For guidelines regarding the writing and teaching of history, see Sita Ram Goel, *The Story of Islamic Imperialism in India,* Voice of India, New Delhi, 1982 reprinted in 1995.

and so on, which did succeed in giving it a vision of its own past. The Vedic literature, the Sangama compilations, the Jainagama, the Tripitaka and the sacred literature of other Hindu sects gave some glorious accounts of heroes who had fought and foiled a variety of villains. The mighty men and women who stalked the scene in this sacred literature had drawn spontaneous response from the deepest in human nature.

Nor was Hindu society lacking in a sense of time-series, though it could not boast of an exact chronology couched in terms of reignal years for every ruling prince. The sheet-anchor of this time-series was cycles of *kalpas, manvantaras*, and *chaturyugas* succeeding each other in an untold spread of creation and destruction. The Puranas provided some salient signposts in the vastness of this world-process—the various *avatāras* who descended in order to destroy the demons that were desecrating the earth with their dismal deeds. The Jainagama and the Tripitaka told a similar story as a succession of *tīrthaṅkaras* and *buddhas* who sought and found the light that could dispel the darkness of ignorance and suffering in every epoch.

This sense of time-series became a little more concise and concrete as the scene shifted to more recent times. The Puranas told the story of Parashurama, Rama Dasharthi, and Krishna Vasudeva in a more detailed manner as these *avatāras* appeared at the end of Satayuga, Treta and Dvapara. With the coming of Kaliyuga in 3102 BC, a count of diverse dynasties was also given, together with the names of kings who succeeded at Ayodhya. Hastinapur, Kashi, Kampilya, Kausambi, Mathura, Mithila and Rajagriha. Finally, with the rise of Magadha to supreme imperial power under the Sisunagas, the Nandas, the Mauryas, the Sungas, the Kanvas, the Andhras and the Guptas, this traditional history acquired a chronology as well.

But what remained significant in all this history was a singular forgetfulness about foreign invasions. The passing episode of a short-lived Iranian inroad was not remembered at all. Nor was the Macedonian adventure except in the word *"yavana"* which became a common denominator for all perpetrators of *adharma.* Vikramaditya was more widely known as the founder of an era and as a just ruler than as Sakari who hurled back the Sakas. The Huna was remembered only as a degenerate *kshatriya* who had fallen from the heroic code of conduct.

HINDUS REMEMBERED ONLY THEIR OWN HEROES

Coming to the period following Islamic invasions, Hindu society did not bother to remember the Arabs, the Ghaznavids, the Ghurids, the

Mamluks, the Khaljis, the Tughlaqs, the Sayyads, the Lodis, and the Mughals. But it took pride in Bapa Raval who had humbled the Arabs; in Maharani Nayakidevi of Gujarat and Prithivi Raj Chauhan who had defeated Muhammad Ghuri again and again; in Gora and Badal who had rescued Rana Ratan Singh from the camp of Alauddin Khalji and then laid down their lives in defence of Padmini and her Chittor; in Harihara and Bukka who had founded the Vijayanagar Empire which stood like a rock against Islamic imperialism for more than two centuries; in Rana Sangram Singh who had crossed swords with Babur; in Maharana Pratap who had defied the mightiest Mughal in the midst of great adversity; in Durgadas Rathor who had despised the wrath of Aurangzeb in defence of his right to give refuge to a rebellious Mughal prince; in Chhatrapati Shivaji who devised a new diplomacy and innovated a new art of warfare which finally worsted the most powerful Muslim empire and rolled back the Islamic invasion; in Chhatrasal Bundela and Maharaja Surajmal who revived Hindu rule in the north; in Banda Bairagi who avenged the wrongs done by Muslim despots to Guru Arjun Deva, Guru Tegh Bahadur and Guru Gobind Singh; and in Maharaja Ranjit Singh who liberated the Punjab and the North-West Frontier Province from Islamic stranglehold.

There are many other local legends of heroes and heroines preserved and perpetuated by provincial poets and story-tellers. The one point that predominated in all this poetry and prose was not a sense of grudge and grievance against the enemies who had wronged Hindu society at different occasions, but a sense of pride that Hindu society had faced every enemy with courage and fortitude, and laid him low at last. This tradition of honouring its own heroes and heroines with no heed paid to invaders and wrong-doers had saved Hindu society from bitterness which works like a poison in the soul, and which ultimately makes a society pugnacious and chauvinist. Hindu society had hardly any time to spare from singing the praises of its own great men and women, and from aspiring to mould its children in their inimitable images.

THE WESTERN VERSION OF INDIAN HISTORY

The British and other Western historians started by dismissing most of this traditional history as 'tall tales told by court poets whose first preference was not truth so much as payments made by princes and patrons'. These tales, we were told, had no basis in facts as recorded by the 'more meticulous' foreign travellers, and as could be corroborated by archaeological, epigraphical and numismatic evidence in India itself. The Itihasa-Purana which Hindu society had so far cherished as its historical literature was summarily dismissed as mere mythology which no 'historian worth his salt' could take seriously. Similarly, the historical literature of later ages was lumped together as bardic braggartism or, at best, as a species of self-consolation on the part of a society which had suffered staggering defeats.

But the most significant part of this 'painstaking research' was not so much the frowning at what was regarded as 'mere fables' as the promotion of what was affirmed as 'sober facts'. The results of this 'research' were very revealing indeed. Hindu society was informed that its so-called hoary history was nothing more than an unrelieved record of foreign invasions before which this society had always made an abject surrender. The factors which had rendered Hindu society so 'supine', were also unravelled, one after another. The 'puerile priestcraft' of the Brahmins which was never repudiated, the caste system which was never questioned, the pessimism of the Jains and the Buddhists which always led to lethargy and lack of spirit — all these were put under the microscope and dissected in detail. The only relieving features of this ' history' were some pieces of epic poetry, some specimens of sculpture, some mysticism, some philosophy, and some rudimentary science.

The 'research' started with the Vedas which Hindu society had never suspected as books of history. The findings in this field were truly formidable. Firstly, it was 'found' that the Vedas did not relate to a remote antiquity as Hindu society had fondly believed so far. On the contrary, all 'available evidence' led to the 'incontrovertible' conclusion that the Vedas were composed around 1200 BC if not much later. Secondly, it was 'discovered' that the Vedas did not contain any lofty spiritual lore as Hindu society had been led to believe by the 'wily Brahmins'. On the contrary, they were compendiums of 'warlike ballads, sordid sorcery, and abject appeals for wealth and victory made to primitive gods by superstitious poets'. Thirdly, it was 'deduced' that the 'Aryans' were not autochthonous to India. On the contrary, they were 'invaders' from the steppes of Central Asia or the forests of Germany and Scandinavia. Fourthly, it was 'proved' that the 'Aryans' were not at all the noble characters portrayed in Jain, Buddhist and classical Sanskrit literature. On the contrary, they were 'blood-thirsty barbarians' who had 'massacred' most of the 'original inhabitants' of India — the Dravidians — and 'driven away' the rest towards the South. No wonder that Hindu society was swept off its feet by these 'scientific findings' and is still searching for a *terra firma* on which it could stand again.

The further unfoldment of this 'research' was still more significant. Hindu society was told that its 'Aryan ancestors' had not only destroyed a rich 'Dravidian civilisation', glimpses of which can be seen at Harappa and Mohenjo-daro and in the Sangama literature, but had also 'opened the floodgates' in the North-West for wave after wave of foreign invaders. The 'Indian sub-continent' was soon invaded by the Iranians under Darius, though he could not complete his 'conquest' because he had to rush back towards the Western ramparts of his empire which were being battered by the 'brave Greeks'. Alexander of Macedonia invaded the 'Indian sub-continent' soon after. *The Cambridge History of India* devotes more pages to this 'Greek invasion' than it does to any other chapter in Indian history. The 'triumphal march' of Alexander's army is traced almost inch by inch as if an event like that had never taken place in the annals of India, before and after.

The Mauryas under Chandragupta 'checkmated' the Greeks for a 'brief interval'. But the 'intrepid' Greeks burst forth again on the Indian scene after the death of Ashoka and could not be stopped by the Sungas in spite of all the 'boasts' which Pusyamitra and his progeny have bequeathed to posterity. The Greeks penetrated as far as Pataliputra in the East and Madhyamika in Central India. They were followed by the Sakas and the Kushanas and the Hunas who wrecked every 'ramshackle empire' which Hindu society had 'managed' to 'patch up' in the meanwhile. On the other hand, these invaders founded some 'famous empires' of their own and ruled over large parts of India for a long time. The 'only thing' that can be said to the 'credit' of Hindu society during this 'dark period' is that it finally succeeded in 'enervating' these 'robust races', as also in absorbing them in its own Brahmanical or Buddhist 'culture'. The 'descendants' of these 'dauntless warriors' came to be known as Rajputs, Jats, Ahirs and Gujars who still constitute whatever 'healthy' elements the 'decadent' Hindu society has managed to retain till our own times.

Finally, Hindu society suffered a 'knock-out blow' at the hands of the Turks, the Pathans and the Persians, and was reduced to 'shambles' from which it has never really recovered. Although these Muslim conquerors 'domiciled' themselves in India and built several 'far-flung empires', they refused to be taken in by the 'old tricks' which Hindu society had played on every earlier conqueror. They despised Hindu religion and culture, destroyed Hindu shrines and scriptures, humiliated Hindu holy men, killed and ate cows, and molested Hindu women on a large scale, without inviting any 'strong or significant reprisals' from Hindu society. They struck such 'terror' in Hindu hearts as to make every Hindu 'tremble' at the very mention of the word 'Muslim'. Had not the British saviours arrived in the 'nick of time', and 'rescued' Hindu society from the morass of Muslim tyranny, this society would have 'gone down the drain of human history' without leaving a trace.

This was the 'main current' of Indian history as told by the British and other Western historians. There were slight variations on the theme, here and there. But, by and large, the burden was that Hindu society had never succeeded in its fight for freedom. In the process, Hindu heroism that fought the Iranians, the Greeks, the Sakas, the Kushanas and the Hunas was reduced to a rearguard action by a people on the retreat. In this perspective, Hindu resistance to Islamic imperialism was reduced to sporadic revolts led by provincial chieftains motivated by petty personal gains. In this context, the counter-attack delivered by Hindu society to defeat and disperse Islamic imperialism was interpreted as an invitation to anarchy. The British could now claim very rightfully that they had inherited India from a decrepit Mughal empire which could not defend itself against 'Maratha brigandage' on the one hand, and against modern methods of diplomacy and warfare on the other.

The national fight for freedom against British imperialism had repudiated this Western version of Indian history, and revived the national historical tradition of not tolerating foreign rule in any part of Bharatavarsha. But by the time the battle against British imperialism drew to a close, the Western version had recaptured the imagination of our leaders most of whom had been educated either in England or in 'native' schools and colleges whose curriculum had been laid down by the British. They failed to see that the Muslim League represented the revival of Islamic imperialism, and came to regard mounting Muslim demands as merely communal complaints. And they trembled every time the Muslim spokesmen threatened them with 'terrible consequences'. They did not allow Hindu society to organize itself, and meet Islamic terrorism at every level, ideological as well physical. And they surrendered abjectly before a force which was no more formidable than frenzied Muslim mobs staging street riots.

CHAPTER IV
THE BUSINESS OF BLAMING THE BRITISH

Problems have to be solved first at the level of thought before we can hope to solve them at the level of things. Hindu society has got to do some hard thinking in order to find an effective and lasting solution of the problem posed by Islam.

ISLAM AND HINDU SOCIETY

Islam came to India as a fully developed ideology of an aggressive and self-righteous imperialism. It tormented Hindu society for several centuries. It should have been demolished and dispersed when its imperialist hold was broken at last, after a long struggle. But it was allowed to survive and its inherent aggressiveness was not tamed. Hindu society had meanwhile deceived itself into believing that Islam was just another religion and, therefore, entitled to reverence.

Islam became an ardent and active accomplice of British imperialism against which Hindu society had to wage another struggle. It made the struggle much more difficult than it would have been otherwise, and coerced the national leadership to do all sorts of political and constitutional acrobatics. Finally, when Hindu society succeeded in winning its freedom again, it forced a partition of the Hindu homeland with the help of a foreign power. Hindu society had to pay this price because it had again deceived itself into believing that Islam could also inspire patriotism, and that the votaries of this creed also deserved an honourable accommodation.

Islam has established its theocratic states on both sides of the truncated homeland which Hindu society has been able to retain for itself. It has driven away millions of Hindus from their ancestral homes, and has been harassing in a most harrowing manner millions of other Hindus who have been unable to escape from its bigotry.

Even inside the truncated Hindu homeland, Islam has been spreading its poison in the whole body politic. It has fomented no end of strife, violence, and vituperation. It has distorted the democratic processes with the weight of its vote-bank. In recent years, it has started corrupting public life with the help of massive finances obtained by it from its neo-rich patrons abroad. And it is again out to decimate Hindu society so that it may acquire a majority and restore its lost empire.

Hindu society should have done some hard thinking about Islam and its invariably vicious behaviour which Hindu society has witnessed for so long and at such great cost to itself. But that is exactly the habit which Hindu society seems to have lost — the habit of hard thinking. For quite some time now, Hindu society has been substituting some soft and soothing slogans in place of hard and creative thought. What is worse, even the slogans it raises are seldom its own. It simply borrows them from wherever they are available in an alluring and facile form.

One such slogan has been that the British sowed the seeds of discord between Hindus and Muslims, and brought about the partition of the country before they left. The slogan was raised by leaders of the Indian National Congress at an early stage of the freedom fight against the British. In course of time, this slogan assumed the status of a dogmatic 'diagnosis' of the 'communal situation' which continued to deteriorate in direct proportion to the pitch at which this slogan was shouted.

It had been observed that the Muslim leadership was not only reluctant to join the national struggle but was also manifesting an increasing hostility to the national movement. Sir Syed Ahmad Khan, the topmost Muslim leader, had questioned not only the national character of the Indian National Congress but also the very concept of Indian nationalism. In his considered opinion, Hindus and Muslims could not live together unless the one conquered and put down the other. The leaders of the Congress went out in search of some Muslim notables who could counter this hostile campaign. They found a few who agreed to preside over the Congress sessions or to speak from its platform. But all these 'Nationalist Muslims' ended by more or less singing the tune set by Sir Syed Ahmad Khan.

This should have made the national leadership sit up and take stock of the situation. A thoughtful way would have been to map out the Muslim psyche, and trace it to its source. The leaders would have discovered without too great an effort that the nation had to fight not only the British but also the residues of Islamic imperialism — Syeds, Sheikhs, Mughals, Pathans, Sufis, Khwajas, Alims, Mujaddids, mullahs, maulvis, muftis, imams, hajis, qutbs and qazis. All these honorifics had been monopolized by the descendants of Arabs, Turks, Iranians and North Africans who had been, at one time or the other, either the swordsmen of Islam or the flunkies of Islamic courts. They had never learnt to do a day's honest work, and had lived lavishly either on booty or on *madad-i-ma'ash* (stipends) made available to them by the plunderers of that booty. These predators and parasites were now trying to retain and tighten their hold over a large segment of the native population which had been lured or forced into the fold of Islam when their forefathers had ruled the roost. The nation had to isolate these residues of Islamic imperialism on the one hand, and to win back the lost sheep of Hindu society on the other. That was the need of the hour and there was no other way out.

A SLOGAN BORROWED FROM THE BRITISH

But Hindu society did not undertake that difficult but necessary task. Instead, it borrowed a slogan, this time from the British themselves, and felt fully satisfied that it had found a way out of the dilemma.

Lord Elphinstone had said as far back as 1851 that "*Divide et empera* was the old Roman motto, and it should be ours". Many other British politicians, historians and bureaucrats, in Britain as well as in India, had made similar statements of British policy. The British had never tried very hard to hide the game they had played in the past, and were planning to play in the future. But the national leaders who read or heard these statements became agog with excitement as if they had uncovered a 'dark secret', and could now answer comfortably all questions regarding the 'communal problem'.

The leaders of the nation lost no time in taking into confidence the 'leaders' of the 'Muslim community'. The message conveyed was that the British imperialists were bent upon breaking the 'bonds between brother and brother', and that Muslims should unite with Hindus to expose and defeat the British game. But Muslim leaders remained far from being impressed by the gravity of the message, or else smiled in utter contempt. On their part, they were finding it much more profitable to negotiate a cold and calculated *quid pro quo* with the British, on the basis of mutual cooperation.

Yet the leaders of the nation did not even suspect that the slogan of *divide et impera* was not at all relevant in the context of Hindu-Muslim relations. Their speeches and writings remained chock-full of the very same slogan. Some of them went to the extent of saying that Hindus and Muslims will shed all mutual hostility and hug one another as soon as the British took leave of India. The policies pursued by the leaders were an integral part of this misreading of the Muslim mind, and led to disaster in due course.

THE SAME SLOGAN IS STILL CURRENT

The British have left. But the relations between Hindus and Muslims are no better, if not worse, than they were during the British rule. This should have been a sufficient proof that the British were only exploiting the differences that already existed between Hindus and Muslims, and that the British had not created those differences.

Yet this slogan gets the pride of place in study after study of Hindu-Muslim relations during the post-1857 and pre-Partition period. The political pundits inform us, with airs of profound insight, how the British 'persecuted' the Muslims and 'patronized' the Hindus in the aftermath of 1857; how they started tilting towards the Muslims and away from the Hindus as soon as the latter showed signs of rebellion; how they made 'mischievous' overtures towards the Muslims by carving a Muslim majority province out of the Presidency of Bengal; how they took advantage of the situation when the Hindus alienated the Muslims by opposing the Partition of Bengal; how they broke the 'joint family' by bringing in separate electorates; how they promoted Muslim separatism till the Muslim League passed its Lahore Resolution; and finally, how they commissioned a master diplomat like Mountbatten to enact the last act in a 'dirty drama'.

These are supposed to be sober and scholarly studies as compared to the 'scientific studies' produced by the Marxist-cum-Muslim 'historians'. This tribe which is now entrenched in every university department of history and political science all over the country, which has come to control all prestigious forums concerned with the writing and teaching of history and social studies, and which enjoys exclusive patronage from the powers that be, has explained away the 'minor faults and follies of the Muslim minority' in terms of the 'major crimes of Hindu communalism'. These 'historians' have firmly fixed the responsibility for Partition on 'Hindu revivalism and reaction' which joined hands with the 'forces of feudalism, capitalism and imperialism' in order to 'drown the toiling masses in mutual bloodshed'. The chickens hatched by the slogan of *divide et impera* have returned home to roost.

A WELCOME DEPARTURE

It is, therefore, a welcome departure from the beaten and the brazen tracks that Shri H.V. Seshadri has not laboured morbidly over British machinations to divide the two communities. Out of as many as 27 chapters in *The Tragic Story of Partition* he has devoted only one chapter to this jejune and jaded theme. In another chapter, Abetting Muslim Separatism, he has made the point quite clear that separatism was the stock-in-trade of Muslim leadership, and that the British only made use of it for their own purposes. The unmistakable impression that is left on one's mind, after one has finished the book, is that it was not the British but the misconceived though well-intentioned policies of the national leadership which cleared the way for a re-consolidation of

Islamic imperialism in the Eastern and Western wings of India.

To an adult mind this whole business of blaming the British for Muslim separatism, which was and is in fact inspired by Islam, must look like an infantile attempt at refusing to accept our own responsibility for our own failures on a strategic front. It is high time for Hindu society to start facing unpleasant realities rather than wish them away by taking resort to plausible explanations.

In this particular instance, the explanation is not even plausible. It falls to the ground as soon as we go beyond the realm of Hindu-Muslim relations, and reflect upon eventual results of the same British policy elsewhere.

FAILURE OF BRITISH POLICY ON ALL OTHER FRONTS

The British had practised their policy of divide-and-rule not only between Hindus and Muslims; they had also tried to set several sections of Hindu society against each other. They had tried to embitter the 'Dravidian South' against the 'Aryan North' by selling the story of an 'Aryan invasion' even to our school-going children. They had encouraged the so-called scheduled castes and scheduled tribes to break away from the so-called caste Hindus. The princes had been isolated from their own people, and 'native India' from 'British India'. The 'martial races' had been demarcated from 'non-martial' communities, and the 'agriculturalist masses' from 'non-agriculturist classes'. The 'non-Brahmins had been instigated against the Brahmins. Some Sikh scholars had been egged upon to protest that the Sikhs were not a section of Hindu society. Resentment had been inspired against 'Bengali imperialism' in Assam, Bihar and Orissa, and against 'Tamil domination' in Kannada, Malayalam and Telegu speaking areas. The cinders of some of those flames ignited by the British continue to fly in our faces every now and then, even after independence.

But when the chips were down and the British got ready to go, all these mutual misgivings were overcome. All segments of Hindu society closed their ranks and stood united like a solid phalanx. It was only the Muslim community which stood apart and stuck out like a sore thumb. The British policy of divide-and-rule had failed everywhere except among the Muslims. We have to find out the facts and forces which made the difference.

FAULTY PERCEPTIONS OF NATIONAL LEADERSHIP

The basic perception that the British policy of divide-and-rule did not make much difference to the Hindu-Muslim relations becomes clear if we reverse the context, and consider those policies which were evolved and pursued by the national leaders themselves entirely on their own, and which went a long way in promoting Partition. The British had absolutely no hand in inspiring or shaping those surrenders which the Indian National Congress made before the Muslim leaders at different stages. And those policies were endorsed by the tallest and the topmost among the national leaders.

Shri Seshadri has listed and commented upon many of these mistaken policies. But those great leaders of a great people have not suffered the slightest diminution in his estimation. He has not cast a single aspersion on their large-heartedness or their good intentions. All that he has done is to point out that good intentions alone are no guarantee of good results, more so when the vision falters due to faulty perceptions or lack of proper reflection.

We may add a word in order to emphasize that a bitter or indignant or value-loaded lament over British policies of divide-and-rule is neither here nor there, even when those policies did cause some great damage. The British had not come to India for picking roses. They had not come to India because they had fallen for her fauna and flora, or her folk dances, or her mysticism and metaphysics. On the contrary, they had come here for the very prosaic purpose of conquering, consolidating and conserving an empire which had proved progressively more profitable to them, and which was soon to catapult them from the status of a second-rate European nation to that of the most formidable world-power. They would not have been worth their salt if they had not played the patent game of all imperialists, in all ages. Blaming the British on that count is tantamount to conceding, in the first instance, the British claim that they had a civilizing mission in India, and then complaining that they had not lived upto that claim. The entire exercise is infantile and extremely puerile.

CHAPTER V
THE FRUSTRATION OF ISLAM IN INDIA

Long ago, some 12 or 13 years before Partition, I had a chance to pass by a meeting of Muslims in Delhi. The chaste Urdu and the weighty voice of the man making the speech at the moment, made me stand and stare. It was a bearded mullah wearing a fez. He was narrating some history which was new for me.

The mullah mentioned several dates on which some decisive battles had been fought and won by the armies of Islam. I was not familiar with the names of the heroes and generals who had led those armies. But I knew the names of the countries which, according to the mullah, had been conquered and converted *en masse* to Islam in rather short spans of time — Arabia, Palestine, Syria, Iraq, Egypt, Algeria, Tunisia, Morocco, Iran, Khorasan, Turkistan and so on. There were repeated references to swords and spears and horses and hoofs and countless clashes in which human blood had flowed copiously. In between, some one from the audience stood up and shouted *'nāra-i-takbīr'*. And the whole assembly roared back *Allāh-o-Akbar* with full-throated frenzy.

Then the speaker moved to Sind and Hind. He recounted the many 'miracles' which Islam had wrought here with the might of its sword as well as the spell of its Sufis, for more than a thousand years. I knew some of those 'miracles' from my own text-books of history, though I had never suspected that they could be made to sound so superhuman as in the mouth of this mullah. And then, all of a sudden, the mullah's voice sank and became almost a whimper. His face too must have fallen, though I could not see it from the distance at which I was standing. He was now telling, in very mournful tones, how Islam had failed to fulfil its mission in this '*kambakht* (unfortunate) *mulk* (country)' which was still crawling with *kufr* (infidelism) in spite of all those arduous endeavours undertaken by the heroes of Islam. A funeral silence fell on the audience, and no one now stood up any more to invite another *nāra-i-takbīr*. I moved away from the meeting and sat down in another part of the same park where the mullah's voice reached me no more. But after some time the atmosphere was rent again by another bout of *Allāh-o-Akbar*. I wondered what spell the mullah had spread over his audience again.

One thing that had puzzled me a good deal in the mullah's speech was his description of the great Gaṅgā as a *dahānā* (rivulet) instead of as a *daryā* (river). I had not seen the Gaṅgā so far with my own eyes.

But my text-books of geography had told me that it was a mighty river, one of the four or five biggest and longest in the world. The mullah's description of it did not fit with a known fact. He was a middle-aged man, and sounded rather well-read in history and geography. I thought that he should have known better.

It was many years later that one day Professor Balraj Madhok cited to me the famous couplet of Altaf Husain Hali in which the Gaṅgā had been contemptuously described as a *dahānā*.[1] I was suddenly reminded of the speech I had heard as a school boy. But by now I had acquired a good knowledge of medieval Indian history. A new image of medieval India had also emerged in my mind by reading K.M. Panikkar's *A Survey of Indian History*. It was no more the India of Muslim monarchs ruling leisurely over a large empire, building mosques and *mazārs* and *madrasas* and mansions, and patronizing poets and other men of letters. On the contrary, it was the story of the long-drawn-out war which took a decisive turn to the disadvantage of Islamic imperialism with the rise of Shivaji. The war had ended in a victory for the Hindus by the middle of the 18th century. A few months earlier, I had finished a Hindi translation of Kincaid's *The Grand Rebel* which I had named *Shaktīputra Shivājī*. I had fully concurred with Kincaid's conclusion that the British had taken over India not from the Muslims but from the Hindus.

Shri H.V. Seshadri has also quoted that couplet of Hali in *The Tragic Story of Partition*.[2] He has also given a brief outline of the long war of liberation which Hindu society had fought and won against Islamic imperialism. He writes: "For 800 years Hindusthan waged a relentless freedom struggle — probably the most stirring saga of crusade for national freedom witnessed anywhere on the face of this earth. From Maharana Kumbha to Maharana Pratap Simha and Rajasimha in Rajasthan, from Hakka and Bukka to Krishnadevaraya in the South, from Chhatrapati Shivaji to the Peshwas in Maharashtra, from the various martyr Gurus of the Sikhs including Guru Govind Singh to Banda Bairagi and Ranjit Singh in the Punjab, from Chhatrasal in Bundelkhand to Lachit Barphukan in Assam, countless captains of the war of independence piloted the ship of freedom and steered her through perilous tides and tempests. As a result of their ceaseless and crushing blows, the conquering sword of Islam lay in dust, shattered to pieces."[3]

---

[1] Hati had mourned in his most famous poem that though the invincible armada of Islam had crossed many mighty rivers and seas, it got drowned in the rivulet that was the Gaṅgā!

[2] *The Tragic Story of Partition*, p. 2.

[3] Ibid., p. 1-2.

TWO VERSIONS OF MEDIEVAL INDIAN HISTORY

Obviously, there is a deep divide between the two versions of medieval Indian history — Hindu and Muslim. Hindu society may like to forget the first phase of this history during which it suffered defeat after defeat in spite of a succession of great heroes who tried to blunt the sword of Islam, and block the path of Islamic invasion. But Hindu society cannot help taking pride in the phase which opened with the rise of Shivaji, and unfolded further under Chhatrasal, Banda Bairagi, Surajmal and Ranjit Singh. On the other hand, the mullah's gaze is galvanized on the period when the sword of Islam swept over the length and breadth of the Hindu homeland. He cannot help feeling humbled when he moves to a later period, and finds the hordes of Islam in hasty retreat before a Hindu counter-attack. The feeling in Hindu society at the end of it all is one of fulfilment; the feeling in the mullah's mind, on the other hand, is one of utter frustration. Islam had suffered in India a second and serious defeat after its first and total rout in Spain.

The political pundits have so far failed to lay their fingers on the forces which led to India's Partition, firstly because they have confined their purview to a brief period of 90 years — from 1857 to 1947. They would have to travel back in time for more than 900 years before they can hope to discover the springs of that deep-seated split — spiritual and cultural — which culminated in the formation of Pakistan. Secondly, they make a serious mistake when they pit a so-called Hindu revivalism against a so-called Muslim revivalism, and put both of them on par as equally guilty parties for making a mess of it all. They would have to undertake a deeper probe into the intrinsic character and inherent dynamics of each 'revivalism', before they can hope to acquire an adequate insight into the interaction of powerful and mutually hostile historical forces.

HINDU AND MUSLIM 'REVIVALISM'

Hindu 'revivalism' in the 19th century was essentially a resurgence of the national spirit of a people who were native to the land, and who had suffered terribly and for a long time from successive foreign invasions. Hindu society was aspiring to reform and renew itself in the image of its ancient ideals which had endowed it with strength and stability and kept it immune from alien inroads. In the process, Hindu society had an inalienable right to pronounce its own judgments on imported ideologies which had coerced and corrupted it, as also on 'heroes' of the histories enacted by its inveterate enemies.

On the other hand, Muslim 'revivalism' was the frenzied reaction of a foreign fraternity which had finally failed to convert a majority of the native population to its own criminal creed, and which was, therefore, feeling terribly frustrated. The diehard descendants of Muslim swordsmen and sufis were now reviving dreams of an empire which their forefathers had built with so much bloodshed but which had been lost in the last round. They were calling upon their confused comrades and converted victims to revert to those medieval mores when Islam had moulded the pagan and peace-loving people of Arabia into a brotherhood of bandits. In the process, they were fast becoming the inmates of a lunatic asylum crowded with some of the most desperate characters.

The history of Arab and Turkish aggressions against India would have been no different from the history of earlier aggressions by the Greeks, the Sakas, the Kushanas, and the Hunas but for the presence of a new factor. A culturally superior and temperamentally compassionate Hindu society would have tamed these latter-day barbarians as well, and turned them into civilized members of its own household. What made the big difference and complicated matters was that the Arabs and the Turks had themselves become victims of the vicious ideology of Islam, and lost their own cultural identity before they came to this country.

THE PRISON-HOUSE OF ISLAMIC THEOLOGY

Islam was born as a totalitarian and terrorist cult, which it has remained ever since. Its only 'religious' achievement was to rationalize the lowest human passions, and stamp them with the supernatural seal of an almighty Allah. It was, therefore, inevitable for it to become an ideology of imperialism with a clean conscience. The followers of Islam thus found it easy to feel convinced that they were carrying out the commandments of Allah while they invaded other countries, indulged in mass slaughter, converted the conquered people by force, misappropriated other people's properties, captured and sold into slavery countless men and women and children, and destroyed every vestige of culture and true spirituality. They could not but regard as legitimate rewards from Allah the loot and the slaves which they took whenever they were victorious.

But what made matters much worse, the same theology prevented the Muslims from coming to terms with reality in moments of defeat. They refused to renounce their claim to ill-gotten gains, and tended to become ever more fanatical and frantic in their efforts to recover what they were made to disgorge. The theology had laid down that Allah had mandated the whole world to the *millat,* and entrusted all its wealth and population to the custody of Islam. How could Allah wish otherwise? Every setback had, therefore, to be interpreted and proclaimed as due to a temporary estrangement of Allah simply because the *millat* had turned away from practising the pieties prescribed by the Prophet and the first four caliphs. The *millat* had only to return to those old mores, and Allah would restore to it whatever he had taken away in a fit of wrath. As the *millat* could not live without Allah, Allah also could not maintain himself without the *millat.* That is how the argument runs in commentary after commentary on the Quran and the Hadis. That is why the *millat* has alternated between a riotous living at other people's expense, and an equally riotous return to piety.

THE PIETY OF ISLAM

There are many myths afloat about the piety of early Islam, particularly among those Hindus who want to prove that Islam is as good a religion as their own. Many people get impressed by the piety exhibited and exhorted by the Mullah and the Sufi. They do not know that Islamic piety has always been an inherent function of Islamic fanaticism. The more pious a Muslim, the more dangerous he becomes for his fellow human beings. It was the piety of Islam which made its swordsmen behave as they did, both in victory and defeat. It was the piety of Islam which installed the Mullah and the Sufi at the centre of the *millat,* and enabled them to control its mind as well as its heart.

When the armies of Islam rode roughshod over the Hindu homeland, the swordsman of Islam was very likely to relax and retreat from callous carnage after some time. He was likely to get satiated after the first few rounds of slaughter and pillage, or feel some sympathy for fellow human beings, or balk at the destruction of beautiful temples and monasteries, or turn away from burning the sacred and secular literature of non-Muslims, or acquire respect for the spirituality and culture of a people who had behaved so differently from his own comrades-in-arms. It was the Mullah and the Sufi who would not let him relax. They threatened him with hell if he tried to turn away from the work assigned by Allah. The more heinous the crimes which a Muslim monarch or mercenary committed, the higher the place in heaven which the Mullah and the Sufi reserved for him. The greater the slaughter and rapine in which a Muslim army indulged, the more plentiful the wines and houris which were promised to the *ghāzīs*.

But the sweep of the sword of Islam could not continue for ever. The Hindus who had been caught unprepared for this sort of 'religion' and this sort of 'heroism', were not made of clay. They organized a resistance for many years, and finally mounted a counter-attack. The swordsman of Islam was a mortal man in spite of all the praises which Muslim historians and poets had heaped upon him for his invincibility. He fell back as soon as he came in contact with equally sharp or superior steel, then threw away his sword, and finally accepted defeat. It was the Mullah and the Sufi who refused to get reconciled to the new reality. They compiled some more commentaries on the Quran and the Hadis and called upon the *millat* to conquer India once again. This time the claim was advanced on no better a basis than the right acquired from an earlier 'conquest'.

Ever since, the Mullah has sedulously maintained and spread the myth of a Muslim empire in India which was 'stolen slyly' by the 'wily' British. As an after-thought, he adds that Islam has a message for India and that its 'spiritual mission' in India is still unfulfilled. Shri Seshadri has quoted a passage from the preface to F.K. Khan Durrani's *Meaning of Pakistan* which reveals the mind of the Mullah. It says: "There is not an inch of the soil of India which our forefathers did not once purchase with blood. We cannot be false to the blood of our forefathers. India, the whole of it, is therefore our heritage and it must be reconquered for Islam. Expansion in the spiritual sense in an inherent necessity of our faith and implies no hatred or enmity towards the Hindus. Rather the reverse. Our ultimate ideal should be the unification of India, spiritually and politically, under the banner of Islam. The final salvation of India is not otherwise possible."[4] Perversity loses all limits once the human mind passes under the spell of Islam. India is to be enslaved again for the 'spiritual salvation' of Hindu society!

There have been many Mullahs and Muslim scholars in India, Pakistan and the wide world of Islam who have been making similar statements, every now and then. The heroics conveyed was heralded by Shah Waliullah, soon after the Mughal empire started crumbling in the first half of the 18th century. It acquired a feverish pitch after Ahmed shah Abdali, whom Waliullah had invited to wipe out the Marathas and the Jats, also failed to save the situation. The heroes of Islam had disappeared. But the heroics had remained.

The harangues of Waliullah and company were addressed not to an advancing army but to a demoralised crowd of stragglers beating a fast

---

[4] Quoted in Ibid., p. 250.

retreat. The retreat would have soon become a rout if the British had not intervened at a critical juncture. The British did not steal any empire from Islam. On the contrary, they saved the residues of Islamic imperialism from being reduced to their real status vis-a-vis a resurgent Hindu society. The residues used the respite to reassemble their ranks, and get ready for another rearguard action. This is the unmistakable impression left on one's mind by a reflective reading of Indian history during that period. The rest is only secularist make-belief relished by the Mullah and the Marxist.

THE 'SPIRITUAL MISSION' OF ISLAM

The 'spiritual mission' of Islam needs no comment. The residues of Islamic imperialism were not in search of spiritual solace which they could share with their 'countrymen'. On the contrary, they were missing the very mundane monopolization of power and pelf which they had enjoyed earlier. This becomes quite clear as one reads the Presidential Address of Janab R.M. Sayani delivered in 1896 at the 12th Session of the Indian National Congress in Allahabad. Speaking of Muslim psychology, he had said: "Before the advent of the British in India, the Musalmans were the rulers of the country. The Musalmans had therefore all the advantages appertaining to it as the ruling class. The sovereigns and the chiefs were their co-religionists and so were the great landlords and great officials. The court language was their own. Every place of trust and responsibility, or carrying influence and high emoluments was by birthright theirs. The Hindus did occupy some position but the Hindus were tenants-at-will of the Musalmans. The Hindus stood in awe of them. Enjoyment and influence and all good things of the world were theirs. By a stroke of misfortune, the Musalmans had to abdicate their position and descend to the level of their Hindu fellow-countrymen. The Hindus, from a subservient state, came into land, offices and other worldly advantages of their former masters. The Musalmans would have nothing to do with anything in which they might have to come into contact with the Hindus."[5]

A spectre had started haunting the residues of Islamic imperialism — the spectre of British withdrawal from India leaving the Muslims to find their natural and normal place in a nation which had regained its freedom and initiative. That explains the pathetic appeals of the Muslim League to the British rulers to divide India before they quit.

---

[5] *History and Culture of the Indian People*, edited by R.C. Majumdar, Volume XI, *The Struggle for Freedom*, Bombay, 1981, pp. 296-97.

Had our national leaders understood the historical situation and had they perceived the paralysis behind the heroics, there would have been no partition, no Pakistan, and no Bangladesh. Why and how the national leaders failed to face and defeat a frustrated Islamic fraternity is a story still to be told.

Chapter VI
ISLAMIC ATAVISM RENAMED MUSLIM REVIVALISM

"He stayed for a good time in Medina," writes Jablani, "and returned to Mecca in 1731, a little before the start of the Hajj season. Of course, he spent the whole month of Ramzan there and its last ten days in seclusion *(itikat)* in the sacred Mosque. During those hours of seclusion many secret truths were made clear to him and he was duly apprised of some difficult problems. Once he saw in a dream that he was the maintainer of the world — *Aaim-uz-Zaman.*"[1]

Professor S.A.A. Rizvi gives some graphic details of this dream described by Shah Waliullah himself in his *Fuyūd al-Harmayn* which he wrote soon after his return to Indian in 1732: "In the same vision he saw that the king of the *kafirs* had seized Muslim towns, plundered their wealth and enslaved their children. Earlier the king had introduced infidelity amongst the faithful and banished Islamic practices. Such a situation infuriated Allah and made Him angry with His creatures. The Shah then witnessed the expression of His fury in the *mala'ala* (a realm where objects and events are shaped before appearing on earth) which in turn gave rise to Shah's own wrath. Then the Shah found himself amongst a gathering of racial groups such as Turks, Uzbeks and Arabs, some riding camels, others horses. They seemed to him very like pilgrims in the Arafat. The Shah's temper exasperated the pilgrims who began to question him about the nature of the divine command. This was the point, he answered, from which all worldly organizations would begin to disintegrate and revert to anarchy. When asked how long such a situation would last, Shah Wali-Allah's reply was until Allah's anger had subsided... Shah Wali-Allah and the pilgrims then travelled from town to town slaughtering the infidels. Ultimately they reached Ajmer, slaughtered the nonbelievers there, liberated the town and imprisoned the infidel king. Then the Shah saw the infidel king with the Muslim army, led by its king, who then ordered that the infidel monarch be killed. The bloody slaughter prompted the Shah to say that divine mercy was on the side of the Muslims."[2]

WALLIULAH'S RECIPE FOR RE-ESTABLISHING ISLAM

Jablani has left us guessing about 'the solutions of some difficult problems' which had been revealed to Shah Waliullah in that dream at

[1] G.N. Jablani, *Life of Shah Waliullah,* Delhi, 1980, p.29

[2] S.A.A. Rizvi, *Shah Wali-Allah and His Times,* Canberra, 1980, p.218.

Mecca. But Rizvi has summarized them in the following words from Waliullah's magnum opus in Arabic, *Hujjat-Allah al-Baligha*: "According to Shah Wali-Allah the mark of the perfect implementation of the Sharia was the performance of jihad. There were people, said the Shah, who indulged in their lower nature by following their ancestral religion, ignoring the advice and commands of the Prophet Mohammed. If one chose to explain Islam to people like this it was to do them a disservice. Force, said the Shah, was the better course — Islam should be forced down their throats like bitter medicine to a child. This, however, was possible only if the leaders of the non-Muslim communities who failed to accept Islam were killed, the strength of the community was reduced, their property confiscated and a situation was created which led to their followers and descendants willingly accepting Islam. Another means of ensuring conversions was to prevent other religious communities from worshipping their own gods. Moreover, unfavourable discriminating laws should be imposed on non-Muslims in matters of rule of retaliation, compensation for manslaughter, and marriage and political matters. However, the proselytization programme of Shah Wali-Allah only included the leaders of the Hindu community. The low class of the infidels, according to him, were to be left alone to work in the fields and for paying jiziya. They like beasts of burden and agricultural livestock were to be kept in abject misery and despair."[3]

Shah Waliullah was son of Shah Abdur Rahim, a sufi who was employed by Aurangzeb for compiling the *Fatāwa-i-Ālamgīrī*. Those who have illusions about Sufism will do well to study this master-piece of the sufi mind. The son was also a sufi. But instead of turning to Rumi or Attar or Hafiz, he chose Sultan Mahmud of Ghazni as his hero. According to the Shah, Mahmud was the greatest figure in the history of Islam after the first four caliphs. He accused the historians of Islam of failing to recognise the fact that Mahmud's horoscope had been identical with that of the Prophet, and that Mahmud had won as many and as significant victories in *jihād* as the Prophet himself.

Waliullah had travelled all the way to Mecca and Medina — a difficult and dangerous undertaking in his days — and studied under half a dozen Sufis and savants of 'Islamic sciences', only to 'discover' and declare what the meanest mullah in the most obscure village mosque in India had been mouthing for more than a thousand years. He himself wrote as many as 43 books between 1732 and 1762 — thirty thoughtful years — only to re-echo the routine ravings of a thousand theologians

[3] Ibid., pp. 285-286.

who had continued to thunder ever since the advent of Islam in this country! He wrote hundreds of letters to his contemporary Muslim monarchs and mercenaries, including Ahmad Shah Abdali, whom he considered to be the saviours of Islam in India, only to convey the conventional Islamic message which all of them had crammed in their cradles — convert of kill the *kāfirs,* humiliate the Hindus, and establish an Islamic state in keeping with the 'holy' commandments of the Quran!

ATAVISM IS NOT REVIVALISM

We Hindus have an interesting saying — *khodā pahāḍ aur niklī chuhiyā* (one went to the extent of excavating a mountain but found only a she mouse). Muslims who have not lost their sense of humour have also a very apt way of describing their die-hard theologians — *mullah kī dōḍ masjid tak* (however long the way a mullah may run, he always ends at the mosque). One cannot help being reminded of a remark by Bernard Shaw when someone reported to him the way Pavlov had developed his theory of the Conditioned Reflex. Shaw had observed: "After torturing a thousand dogs, he has found what every bitch-trainer in Europe knows."

Hindus who are enamoured of Islamic monotheism, are invited to contemplate the character of Allah as he emerges from the writings of Waliullah. Hindus who credit Islam with the concepts of human brotherhood and social equality, are invited to learn from Waliullah the correct meanings of these concepts according to the scriptures of Islam.

On the other hand, Muslims who often quote the Quranic verse — Let there be no compulsion in religion (II.257) — are invited to repudiate Waliullah, and affirm that he has misrepresented Allah and the Last Prophet. Muslims who proclaim that Islam stands for human brotherhood and social equality are invited to pronounce that Waliullah went against the fundamentals of their faith when he wrote what he did.

We can cite a hundred books, written by modern scholars, hailing Waliullah as one of the half a dozen topmost interpreters of true Islam, and as a veritable messiah for a 'moribund' Muslim society. Professor Aziz Ahmad voices the Muslim consensus on Waliullah when he writes that this man "forms a bridge between medieval and modern Islam in India."[4] All Muslim scholars are agreed that Waliullah was the inaugurator of 'Muslim Revivalism' in the 18th century.

The word 'revivalism' like the word 'communalism' has acquired a bad odour in India's political parlance. Most Hindu scholars have

---

[4] Aziz Ahmad, *Studies In Islamic Culture,* Oxford, 1964, p.204.

come to share this repugnance. Muslim scholars, on the other hand, have no objection to the use of this word in a derogatory sense, so long as it is hurled at Brahmo Samaj, Arya Samaj, Bankim Chandra, Swami Vivekananda, Lokmanya Tilak, Sri Aurobindo, Madan Mohan Malaviya, and Mahatma Gandhi. But they have strong reservations when the same treatment is extended to Waliullah (1703-1762), Syed Ahmad Barelvi (1786-1831), Shariatullah (1790-1831), Sir Syed Ahmad Khan (1817-1898), and Sir Muhammad Iqbal (1876-1938), to name only the most notable spokesmen of Islam after the break-down of the 'Muslim Empire' in India. In such a contingency, they return to the normal and morally positive meaning of revivalism. We shall, therefore, use this word in the sense in which the Muslim scholars use it for their own heroes.

The dictionaries define the word 'revival' as follows — "recovering from languor, neglect, depression, etc; renewed performance, renewed interest or attention; a time of extraordinary religious awakening or working up of excitement especially accompanied by extravagance." None of these meanings fits the fulminations of Waliullah. The phrase 'Muslim Revivalism,' as applied to his labours by Muslim scholars is a misnomer. He may be reproached for repeating *ad nauseam* what his predecessors in the prison-house of Islamic theology had prescribed; but he cannot be accused of reviving anything which had fallen into abeyance for want of ardent advocates.

Have a look at the history of Islamic theology in India till the time of Waliullah. It might have suffered from many logical fallacies. But it had never suffered from the psychological lapses of languor, neglect and depression, etc. It had always been alive and kicking, alert and aggressive.

Study the lives of Islamic theologians in India till their ranks were joined by this new "luminary". They might not have put up any spectacular philosophical performance. But they had not pulled any punches in their polemics against Hindu spirituality, culture and society. Their ringing calls for a renewal of Islam by ruining the Hindus had always gone out in an unmistakable language.

Survey the far-flung Sufi *silsilās* till Waliullah came forward to synthesize them all in the service of Islam in India. The Sufis might not have taken any interest in their own self-improvement; they might not have paid any attention to the abundance of sterling spirituality which surrounded them in the lives of Hindu sages and saints. But few of them had so far failed to curse the Hindu *kāfirs* and consign even the greatest among the Hindu saints to an eternal hell-fire.

Compile a list of civil commotions in the cities that had passed under the control of Islam till Waliullah started writing his long letters to his contemporary military commanders. The Muslim mobs in these places might have missed a religious awakening — ordinary or extraordinary — because of continued brainwashing by the Mullahs and the Sufis. But they had seldom missed the excitement and extravagance of street riots, whenever the Hindu populace had tried to perform its religious rites.

It, therefore, goes to the credit of Shri H.V. Seshadri that he steers clear of the meaningless phrase — Muslim Revivalism — in *The Tragic Story of Partition.* He states in his chapter on Muslim Separatism that Waliullah was only continuing, under changed circumstances, an old Islamic crusade against the Hindus. Shri Seshadri does something more which is equally significant. He links up Waliullah and his latter-day followers — Syed Ahmad Barelvi and Shariatullah, etc. — with Sir Syed Ahmad Khan of the Aligarh Movement, under whom the residues of Islamic imperialism started revising their strategy after years of tilting their blunted swords against the windmills of British imperialism. The British had heaved a sigh of relief, even though the *jihād* of Dudhu Mian (1819-1860) and Titu Mian (1782-1831) etc., had never been more than a marginal nuisance for them. Henceforward, the residues of Islamic imperialism were to be a nuisance for Indian nationalism, till they succeeded in securing their first pound of flesh in the shape of Pakistan.

AN OUTLINE OF ISLAMIC CRUSADE IN INDIA

Shri Seshadri has not given a detailed description of the earlier Islamic crusade which Waliullah had merely continued. Instead, he has chosen to give glimpses of the national fight for freedom which had finally defeated the foe. That is as it should be. The less we brood over black evils of the past, the lighter we feel and the better we become for facing tasks in the present. It is only because Muslim separatism is still a festering sore in our body politic that one has to go back to its sources in an earlier age when the first Muslim army had stepped forward on the soil of India.

Professor Aziz Ahmad has narrated in the following words the encomiums heaped on Mahmud Ghaznavi by the Sufis and Mullahs: "Mahmud of Ghazna's invasion of what was regarded as pagan India was a sensational novelty at the end of the 10th century. The sack of Somnat and the destruction of its temple came to be considered a specially pious exploit because of its analogy in the past with the destruction of the idols of the pagan Arabs by the Prophet. This led to invention of popular legends giving Mahmud's invasion a status of sanctity; and it explains the idealisation of Mahmud by Nizam al-Mulk Tusi and the ideal treatment he has received from earlier Sufi poets like Sanai and Attar, not to mention such collectors of anecdotes as Awfi."[5]

The Sufis and Mullahs had streamed towards India from all over the then Islamic world soon after the first Sultanate was established at Delhi in the first decade of the 13th century. The stream became a swollen flood after the Mongol uprising against Islamic aggression in Central Asia. The Mongols had started giving to the Muslims a stiff dose of the latter's own medicine. They had sacked most of the Muslim citadels and cities in Transoxiana, Khurasan and Iran. Finally, in 1258 A.D., they had destroyed the *Dār-ul-Khilāfat* at Baghdad, and killed the *Amīr-ul-Mu'minīn* in a merciless manner. Many Mullahs and Sufis had fattended for long in these Muslim metropolises on the plundered wealth brought in by the armies of Islam. Their harems were brimful of beautiful maidens and beardless boys captured by Muslim swordsmen in *jihāds* against infidel lands, or brought by Muslim slave merchants in slave markets all over Islamdom. Now, all of a sudden, they had to run in all directions to save their lives. Quite a few of them found a safe haven in the cities and towns of North India which had meanwhile been garrisoned by the armies of Islam.

Had these saints and scholars of Islam been normal human beings, they would have been shaken by their harrowing experience at the hands of the Mongols. The wrongs that had been heaped upon their countries and compatriots would have, in that case, moved them to stand against similar treatment being meted out to their fellow human beings elsewhere. They would have sought to humanize their theology by revising the premises on which their prophet had raised it.

But, unfortunately for them as for India, most of them had become unbalanced by years of mugging up the conventional Islamic lore in *madrasas* and *khānqahs*. The Sufis in particular had poisoned their hearts and heads to an incurable point by meditating morbidly on the gangster masquerading as God in the Quran. They found it impossible to break out of the lunatic asylum in which they had lived for so long. Instead of interpreting the Mongol atrocities as a nemesis for the wrongs done by the Muslims in the past, in many countries, they looked at it all as Allah's *qahr* (wrath) on a *millat* which had fallen from the piety of early Islam! Thus they ended by stamping out what-

[5] Ibid., p.79

ever little softening and sophistication Islam had undergone due to centuries of contact with superior cultures — Greek, Zoroastrian, Chinese, and Hindu-Buddhist.

In the next two centuries, this Sufi-cum-Mullah cartel spread over Central and Southern India in the wake of victorious Muslim arms. Many new *madrasas* and *khānqhas* sprang up on the ruins of temples and monasteries which the Muslim swordsmen had sacked. Islamic theology became more self-righteous as the battles won by superior steel were supposed to have been won by a superior doctrine. Ever since, this theology has remained fossilized in all its fundamentals, and every effort on the part of enlightened Muslims has so far failed to find a chink in its armour.

COMMON CHARACTERISTICS OF ISLAMIC THEOLOGIANS

The list is long of the Sufis and the Mullahs who pressed the war-weary Muslim monarchs to wipe out *kufr* (infidelity) and *shirk* (polytheism) from the face of India. Space does not permit us to summarize the individual performance of even the most prominent members of this large tribe which flourished throughout what is paraded as the Muslim period of Indian history. We will have to be content with describing a few characteristics which they shared in common.

1. All of them came from foreign countries already conquered by Islam and secured lucrative offices or liberal *madad-i-ma'ash* (state stipends) in a state presided over by sultans. They lived in spacious mansions or sprawling *khānqahs* endowed with lands and enriched by sumptuous shares in the loot collected by Muslim armies. Quite a few of them were corrupt and sold junior offices for a consideration, or befooled the believing Muslim masses with a variety of tricks dressed up as miracles;
2. All of them affected longish names prefixed and suffixed by a variety of honorifics, with quite a few *bin* (son of) and *al* (of) in between. They tried to trace their ancestry to Ali and Fatima, or to other close relatives and companions of the Prophet;
3. Most of them wrote commentaries on the Quran or the Hadis or on earlier commentaries of this or that theological or sufi school. There was always a rat race among them to secure larger and larger slices of *madad-i-ma'ash* from the king as well as the courtiers. Quite often, the presents they received from their patrons included helpless Hindu women captured from conquered provinces, or brought in the slave markets.
4. Most of them had stayed in Mecca and Medina for short or long

periods before they arrived in India, or performed a pilgrimage at a later stage. Their zeal for Islam and hatred for the Hindus received a new lease of life after they had studied under similar scholars and saints in the schools of Hijaz;

5. All of them saw visions and dreamt dreams in which they communicated directly with the Prophet, or his progeny, or the four pious caliphs. This was how they received their confirmed commands for reviving Islam by a renewed slaughter of Hindus;
6. Quite a few of them confided to their close disciples that they had also received revelations which compared quite favourably with those contained in the Quran. Some of them were convinced that they too were prophets in their own right, but could not publicize the secret for fear of being beheaded by a sultan, or getting killed by a Muslim mob instigated by rival claimants. So they ended by decorating themselves with slightly less lofty titles — *walī* (friend of Allah), *ghaus* (axis), *qutb* (guide), *qayyūm* (stabilizer), *mujaddid* (renewer), *mahdi* (the great leader who appears on the Last Day), *abdāl, autād, nuqta, akhyār,* and the rest.
7. All of them quarrelled continuously over a thousand themes in their theology. But they never failed to present a prompt agreement whenever they were consulted about the treatment to be meted out to the Hindus. The formula was fool-proof — convert the Hindus by force; kill those Hindus who refuse to recite the *kalima;* slaughter the Brahmins and eat the cows; burn Hindu scriptures; demolish Hindu temples and monasteries; and desecrate places of Hindu pilgrimage in order to humiliate the Hindus; impose draconian disabilities and discriminatory taxes on the Hindus in order to force them into the fold of Islam.

MOST SUFIS WERE HARD-HEARTED FANATICS

Many Hindus have been misled, mostly by their own soft-headed scholars, to cherish the fond belief that the Sufis were spiritual seekers, and that unlike the Mullahs, they loved Hindu religious lore and liked their Hindu neighbours. The Chishtiyya Sufis in particular have been chosen for such fulsome praise. The orthodox among the Muslims protest that the Sufis are being slandered. But the Hindus remain convinced that they themselves know better. Professor Aziz Ahmad is a renowned scholar of Islam in India. He clinches the matter in the following words: "In Indian sufism anti-Hindu polemics began with Muin al-din Chishti. Early Sufis in the Punjab and early Chishtis devoted themselves to the task of conversion on a large scale. Missionary activity slowed down under Nizam al-din Auliya, not because of any new concept of eclecticism, but because he held that the Hindus were generally excluded from grace and could not be easily converted to Islam unless they had the opportunity to be in the company of the Muslim saints for considerable time."[6]

Of course, the Auliya who lived in a sprawling *khānqah* and received rich gifts out of plunder was convinced that he himself was such a Muslim saint. His temper and teachings can be known easily from the writings of Amir Khusru, the poet, and Ziauddin Barani, the historian. Both of them were leading disciples of the Auliya. Both of them express a great hatred for Hindus, and regret that the Hanafi school of Islamic Law had come in the way of wiping out completely the "curse of infidelism" from the face Hindustan.

A similar Sufi saint who died a mere 79 years before Waliullah's birth, was Ahmad Sirhindi (1564-1624). He was always foaming at the mouth against Akbar's policy of peace with the Hindus. He proclaimed himself the *Mujaddid-i-alf-i-sānī,* 'renovator of the second millennium of Islam'. Besides writing several books, he addressed many letters to several powerful courtiers in the reign of Akbar and Jahangir. His *Maktūbāt-i-Imām Rabbānī* have been collected and published in three volumes. According to Professor S.A.A. Rizvi, "'Shariat can be fostered through the sword' was the slogan he raised for his contemporaries."[7]

A few specimens should suffice to show the quality of this man's mind. In letter No. 163 he wrote: "The honour of Islam lies in insulting *kufr* and *kafirs.* One who respects the *kafirs* dishonours the Muslims... The real purpose of levying *jiziya* on them is to humiliate them to such an extent that they may not be able to dress well and to live in grandeur. They should constantly remain terrified and trembling. It is intended to hold them under contempt and to uphold the honour and might of Islam." In Letter No. 81 he said: "Cow-sacrifice in India is the noblest of Islamic practices. The *kafirs* may probably agree to pay *jiziya* but they shall never concede to cow-sacrifice." After Guru Arjun Deva had been tortured and done to death by Jahangir, he wrote in letter No. 193 that "the execution of the accursed *kafir* of Gobindwal is an important achievement and is the cause of the great defeat of the Hindus."[8]

---

[6] Ibid., p. 134.

[7] S.A.A. Rizvi, *Muslim Revivalist Movements in Northern India in the Sixteenth and Seventeenth Centuries,* Agra, 1965, p.247.

[8] Ibid., pp. 248-249.

Sirhindi ranks with Shah Waliullah as one of the topmost sufis and theologians of Islam. Referring to his role, Maulana Abul Kalam Azad has written in his *Tazkirah* that "but for these letters Muslim nobles would not have stood by Islam and but for the efforts of Shaikh Ahmad, Akbar's heterodoxy would have superseded Islam in India."[9] Later on, when K.A. Nizami published a collection of Shah Walilullah's letters addresed to various Muslim notables including Ahmad Shah Abdali, he dedicated it to Maulana Azad. The Maulana wrote back, "I am extremely happy that you have earned the merit of publishing these letters. I pray from the core of my heart that Allah may bless you with the felicity of publishing many books of a similar kind."[10] That should give us a measure not only of 'Muslim Revivalism' but also of many Maulanas who masqueraded as ardent nationalists in order to fight the battle for Islam from within the Indian National Congress.

APPENDIX

It is strange that most of the present-day Muslim scholars refuse to cite the actual statements made about Hindus and Hinduism by their heroes such as Ahmad Sirhindi and Shah Waliullah while praising them to the skies as saviours of Islam in India. Maulana Abul Kalam Azad and Allama Iqbal are shining examples of this intriguing silence. The late Professor Ishtiaq Husain Qureshi published two significant books on the history of Islam in India — *Ulema in Politics* (1972), and *The Muslim Community of the Indo-Pakistan Subcontinent* (1977). He has devoted many pages to Ahmad Sirhindi and Shah Waliullah in both the books. But he has not cited a single sentence written or spoken by the 'great sufis' on how they looked at Hindus and Hinduism. I have no doubt that Nizami has also suppressed those letters of Shah Waliullah in which the latter has poured out his heart about *kufr* and the *kāfirs*. It is only Professor S.A.A Rizvi who has taken us into the secret chambers so to say. Professor Rizvi is a Shia. And the venom which characters like Ahmad Sirhindi have poured on Hindus and Hinduism is quite comparable to that which they poured out on Shias and Shiism.

Professor Rizvi has cited select passages from the original Persian of Ahmad Sirhindi's letters. It is only recently that the letters have become available in Urdu translation. Ahmad Sirhindi wrote to many

---

[9] Ibid., p. 215.

[10] Cited in the Preface to Khaliq Ahmad Nizami, *Shāh Walīullah Dehlvī ke Siyāsī Makhtūbāt,* Second Edition, Delhi, 1969, p. 5.

Muslim notables in the reign of Akbar and Jahangir. Some of these letters were in strong protest against Akbar's policies vis-a-vis Hindus. One of Sirhindi's patrons was Abdul Rahim Khan-i-Khanan whom many Hindus cherish as a Hindi poet and a devotee of Sri Krishna. It is unfortunate that quite a few recipients of these letters cannot be identified straight away because they are addressed by their titles and not by their names. As the letters are not dated, it is difficult to say whether the bearer of a particular title belonged to the reign of Akbar or Jahangir. The same title was given to several persons in succession. I reproduce below some passages from these significant letters in order to show how the mind of this great sufi functioned. He was the leading light of the Naqshbandi sufi *silsilā*, and the foremost disciple of Khwaja Baqi Billah who brought this *silsilā* to India in the reign of Akbar. I may add that the Prophet appeared quite frequently to both Baqi Billah and Ahmad Sirhindi in their dreams or states of trance, and gave guidance to them. We reproduce below some of his statements.

1. It is said that the Shariat prospers under the shadow of the sword (*al-Shara' tahat al-saif*). And the glory of the holy Shariat depends on the kings of Islam....[11]

2. Islam and infidelity (*kufr*) contradict one another. To establish the one means eradicating the other, the coming together of these contradictories being impossible. Therefore, Allah has commanded his Prophet to wage war (*jihād*) against the infidels, and be harsh with them. The glory is Islam consists in the humiliation and degradation of infidels and infidelity. He who honours the infidels, insults Islam. Honouring (the infidels) does not mean that they are accorded dignity, and made to sit in high places. It means allowing them to be in our company, to sit with them, and talk to them. *They should be kept away like dogs.* If there is some worldly purpose or work which depends upon them, and cannot be served without their help, they may be contacted while keeping in mind all the time that they are not worthy of respect. The best course according to Islam is that they should not be contacted even for worldly purposes. Allah has proclaimed in his Holy Word (Quran) that they are his and his Prophet's enemies. And mixing with these enemies of Allah and his Prophet or showing affection for them, is one of the greatest crimes...

...The abolition of *jizyah* in Hindustan is a result of friendship which (Hindus) have acquired with the rulers of this land... What right

[11] *Maktūbāt-i-Imām Rabbānī* translated into Urdu by Maulana Muhammad Sa'id Ahmad Naqshbandi, Deoband, 1988, Volume I, p.211. Emphases added. This letter was written to the Khan-i-Azam of that time.

have the rulers to stop exacting *jizyah?* Allah himself has commended imposition of *jizyah* for their (infidels') humiliation and degradation. What is required is their disgrace, and the prestige and power of Muslims. *The slaughter of non-Muslims means gain for Islam...* To consult them (the *kāfirs*) and then act according to their advice means honouring the enemies (of Islam), which is strictly forbidden...

The prayer (=goodwill) of these enemies of Islam is false and fruitless. It should never be called for because it can only add to their numbers. If the infidels pray, they will surely seek the intercession of their idols, which is taking things too far... *A wise man has said that unless you become a maniac (dīwānah) you cannot attain Islam.* The state of this mania means going beyond considerations of profit and loss. Whatever one gains in the service of Islam should suffice...[12]

3. Ram and Kirshan whom Hindus worship are insignificant creatures, and have been begotten by their parents... Ram could not protect his wife whom Ravan took away by force. How can he (Ram) help others?.... It is thousands of times shameful that some people should think of Ram and Kirshan as rulers of all the worlds... *To think that Ram and Rahman are the same, is extremely foolish.* The creator and the creature can never be one... The controller of the Cosmos was never called Ram and Kirshan before the latter were born. What has happened after their birth that they have come to be equated with Allah, and the worship of Ram and Kirshan is described as the worship of Allah? May Allah save us!

Our prophets who number one lakh and twenty-four thousand have encouraged the created ones to worship the Creator... The gods of the Hindus (on the other hand) have encouraged the people to worship them (the gods) instead... They are themselves misguided, and are leading others astray... See, how the (two) ways are different![13]

4. Before that *kāfir* [Guru Arjun Deva] was executed this recluse [meaning himself] had seen in a dream that the reigning king had smashed the skull of idolatry. Indeed, he was a great idolater, and the leader of the idolaters, and the chief of unbelievers. May Allah blast him! The Holy Prophet who is the ruler of religion as well as the world, has cursed the idolaters as follows in some of his prayers — "O Allah, demean their society, create divisions in their ranks, destroy their

---

[12] Ibid., pp.388-89. Emphasis added. There are several other letters written to other notables in the same strain. This letter was written to Shaikh Farid *alias* Nawab Murtaza Khan who was opposed to Akbar's religious policy, and who supported Jahangir's accession after taking from the latter a promise that Islam will be upheld in the new reign.

[13] Ibid., p.396. Emphasis added. This letter was written to Hirday Ram Hindu who had "expressed affinity" with Sirhindi's school of thought.

homes, and get at them like the mighty one."

It is required by religion [Islam] that *jihād* should be waged against the unbelievers, and that they should be dealt with harshly... It is obligatory on Muslims to acquaint the king of Islam with the evil customs of false religions... Maybe the king has no knowledge of these evil customs... Some Ulama of Islam should come forward, and proclaim the evils present in their (unbelievers') ways... It will be no excuse on the Day of Judgment that they did not proclaim the tenets of the Shariat because they were not called upon (to do so)...[14]

5. The Shariat prevails under the shadow of the sword (*al Shara' tahat al-saif*) — according to this (saying), the Shariat can triumph only with the help of mighty kings and their good administration. But for some time past this saying has been languishing, which means inevitably that Islam has become weak. The unbelievers (Hindus) of Hindustan are demolishing mosques, and erecting their own places of worship on the same sites. There was a mosque in the tank of Kurukhet (Kurukshetra) at Thanesar, as also the tomb of some (Muslim) saint. These have been demolished, and a huge *gurudwārā* has been constructed on the same sites. Besides, the *kāfirs* are holding many celebrations of *kufr*....

It is a thousand pities that the reigning king is a Mussalman, and we recluses find ourselves helpless. There was a time when Islam stood glorified due to the might and prestige of its kings, and the Ulama and the Sufis were honoured and held in high regard. It was with their help that the kings made the Shariat prevail. I have heard that one day Amir Taimur was passing through the bazar at Bukhara when, by chance, the inmates of Khwaja Naqshbandi's *khānqah* were beating the dust out of the mats used in that place. Because Islam was intact in Amir Taimur, he stopped at that spot and regarded the dust of the *khānqah* as musk and sandal. He met a good end.[15]

6. Therefore, it is necessary that infidelity should be cursed in order to serve the faith (Islam). Cursing unbelief in the heart is the lesser way. The greater way is to curse it in the heart as well as with the body. In short, cursing means to nourish enmity towards enemies of the true faith, whether that enmity is harboured in the heart when there is fear of injury from them (infidels), or it is harboured in the heart as well as served with the body when there is no fear of injury from them.

In the opinion of this recluse, there is no greater way to obtain the

---

[14] Ibid., pp.435-36. This letter was written to Shaikh Farid.

[15] Ibid., Volume II, p.1213. This letter was written to Mir Muhammad Nu'man, obviously in the reign of Akbar.

blessings of Allah than to curse the enemies of the faith (be impatient with them). For Allah himself harbours enmity towards the infidels and infidelity...

Once I went to visit a sick man who was close to death. When I meditated on him, I saw that his heart was layered with darknesses. I intended to remove those darknesses. But he was not yet ready for it... When I meditated more deeply, I discovered that those darknesses had gathered due to his friendship with the infidels. They could not be dispersed easily. He had to suffer torments of hell before he could get purged of them...[16]

7. Every person cherishes some longing in his heart. The only longing which this recluse (meaning himself) cherishes is that the enemies of Allah and his Prophet should be roughed up. The accursed ones should be humiliated, and their false gods disgraced and defiled. I know that Allah likes and loves no other act more than this. That is why I have been encouraging you again and again to act in this way. Now that you have yourself arrived at that place, and have been appointed to defile and insult that dirty spot and its inhabitants, I feel grateful for this grace (from Allah). There are many who go to this place for pilgrimage. Allah in his kindness has not inflicted this punishment on us. After giving thanks to Allah, you should do your best to ruin that place and their false gods ... whether the idols are carved or uncarved. Let us hope that you will not act slow. Physical weakness and severity of the cold weather, comes in my way. Otherwise, I would have presented myself, and helped you in doing the job. I would have liked to participate in the ceremony and mutilate the stones...[17]

II

Shah Waliullah also was full of the poison which goes by the name of Islam. But by the time be arrived on the scene, the situation for Islamic imperialism in India had become desperate. Forces of Indian nationalism had risen all over the country, and Islamic imperialism was on a fast retreat. I am reproducing some portions from those letters of Waliullah in which he is making frantic appeals to the swordsmen of Islam for retrieving the situation. It is significant that whole passages of the Persian originals have been dropped from the Urdu translations.

---

[16] Ibid., Volume III, pp. 660-63. These passages are from a long letter in which Ahmad Sirhindi answered a large number of questions from his disciples.

[17] Ibid., pp.707. This letter was also written to Shaikh Farid *alias* Nawab Murtaza Khan who had reached Kangra in November 1620 to conquer the fort and desecrate its temples. Jahangir had followed the Nawab in order to celebrate the victory by sacrificing cows and building a mosque where none had existed before.

Those passages contain the obscene swear-words of which every language of Islam is brimful.

1. ***Letter to Ahmad Shah Abdali, Ruler of Afghanistan***

The presence of the kings of Islam is a great blessing from Allah... You should know that the country of Hindustan is a large land. In olden days, the kings of Islam had struggled hard and for long in order to conquer this foreign country. They could do it only in several turns....[18]

Every (Muslim) king got mosques erected in his territory, and created *madrasas*. Muslims of Arabia and Ajam (non-Arab Muslim lands) migrated from their own lands and arrived in these territories. They became agents for the publicity and spread of Islam here. Uptil now their descendants are firm in the ways of Islam....[19]

Among the non-Muslim communities, one is that of the Marhatah (Maratha). They have a chief. For some time past, this community has been raising its head, and has become influential all over Hindustan...[20]

...It is easy to defeat the Marhatah community, provided the *ghāzīs* of Islam gird up their loins and show courage...[21]

In the countryside between Delhi and Agra, the Jat community used to till the land. In the reign of Shahjahan, this community had been ordered not to ride on horses, or keep muskets with them, or build fortresses for themselves. The kings that came later became careless, and this community has used the opportunity for building many forts, and collecting muskets...[22]

In the reign of Muhammad Shah, the impudence of this community crossed all limits. And Surajmal, the cousin of Churaman, became its leader. He took to rebellion. Therefore, the city of Bayana which was an ancient seat of Islam, and where the Ulama and the Sufis had lived for seven hundred years, has been occupied by force and terror, and Muslims have been turned out of it with humiliation and hurt...[23]

...Whatever influence and prestige is left with the kingship at present, is wielded by the Hindus. For no one except them is there in the ranks of managers and officials. Their houses are full of wealth of all varieties. Muslims live in a state of utter poverty and deprivation. The story is long and cannot be summarised. What I mean to say is that

[18] Translated from the Urdu version of K.A. Nizami, *Shāh Walīullah Dehlvī ke Siyāsī Maktūbāt*, Second Edition, Delhi, 1969, p.83.
[19] Ibid., p.84.
[20] Ibid., p.85.
[21] Ibid., p.86.
[22] Ibid., p.87.
[23] Ibid.

the country of Hindustan has passed under the power of non-Muslims. In this age, except your majesty, there is no other king who is powerful and great, who can defeat the enemies, and who is farsighted and experienced in war. It is your majesty's bounden duty *(farz-i-ain)* to invade Hindustan, to destroy the power of the Marhatahs, and to free the down-and-out Muslims from the clutches of non-Muslims. Allah forbid, if the power of the infidels remains in its present position, Muslims will renounce Islam and not even a brief period will pass before Muslims become such a community as will no more know how to distinguish between Islam and non-Islam. This will be a great tragedy. Due to the grace of Allah, no one except your majesty has the capacity for preventing this tragedy from taking place.

We who are the servants of Allah and who recognise the Prophet as our saviour, appeal to you in the name of Allah that you should turn your holy attention to this direction and face the enemies, so that a great merit is added to the roll of your deeds in the house of Allah, and your name is included in the list of *mujāhidīn fi Sabīlallah* (warriors in the service of Allah). May you acquire plunder beyond measure, and may the Muslims be freed from the stranglehold of the infidels. I seek refuge in Allah when I say that you should not act like Nadir Shah who oppressed and suppressed the Muslims, and went away leaving the Marhatahs and the Jats whole and prosperous.

The enemies have become more powerful after Nadir Shah, the army of Islam has disintegrated, and the empire of Delhi has become childrens' play. Allah forbid, if the infidels continue as at present, and Muslims get (further) weakened, the very name of Islam will get wiped out.[24]

...When your fearsome army reaches a place where Muslims and non-Muslims live together, your administrators must take particular care. They must be instructed that those weak Muslims who live in the countryside should be taken to towns and cities. Next, some such administrators should be appointed in towns and cities as would see to it that the properties of Muslims are not plundered, and the honour of no Muslim is compromised.[25]

2. ***To Najibuddaulah, the Ruhela Ally of Abdali in India***

Your solemn letter has reached (me)...

At the 'hidden level' (occult word), the downfall of the Marhatahs

---

[24] Ibid., pp.90-91.

[25] Ibid., p.92. There is more than a hint that Hindus alone should be plundered and dishonoured.

and the Jats has been decided. Now, therefore, it is only a matter of time. As soon as the servants of Allah gird up their loins and come out with courage, the magic fortress of falsehood will be shattered...[26]

3. ***To Najibuddaulah***

...There are three groups in Hindustan which are known for the qualities of fanaticism and zeal. So long as these three are not exterminated, no king can feel secure, nor any noble. The people (read Muslims) also will not be able to live in peace.

Religious as well as worldly interests dictate that soon after winning the war with the Marhatahs, you should turn towards the forts of the Jats, and conquer them with the blessings from the hidden (occult) world. Next is the turn of the Sikhs. This group should also be defeated, while waiting for grace from Allah.

...I appeal to you in the name of Allah and his Prophet that you should not cast your eye on the property of any Muslim. If you take care in this regard, there is hope that the doors of victory will be opened to you one after another. But if this caution is ignored, I fear that the wails of the oppressed may become obstacles in the way towards your goal.[27]

4. ***To Najibuddaulah***

These words are being written in reply to the verbal message sent by you. I have been asked (by you) to tell (you) about suppression of the rebellion of Jats in the environs of Delhi.

The fact is that this recluse (meaning himself) has witnessed in the occult world the downfall of the Jats in the same way as that of the Marhatahs. I have also seen it in a dream that Muslims have taken possession of the forts and the country of the Jats, and that Muslims have become masters of those forts and that country as in the past. Most probably, the Ruhelas will occupy those Jat forts. This has been determined and decided in the most secret world. This recluse has not the shadow of a doubt about that. But the way that victory will be achieved is not yet clear. What is needed is prayers from those special servants of Allah who have been chosen for this purpose.

...But keep one thing in your mind, namely, that the Hindus who are apparently in your's and your government's employ, are inclined

[26] Ibid., p.103. Shah Waliullah claimed and his devotees believed that he could contact hidden levels of existence and foresee future events. He was often consulted by leading Muslims for finding out his foresights. This letter was obviously written after the defeat of the Marathas in 1761 AD.

[27] Ibid., pp.104-05.

towards the enemies in their hearts. They do not want that the enemies be exterminated. They will try a thousand tricks in this matter, and endeavour in every way to show to your honour that the path of peace is more profitable.

Make up your mind not to listen to this group (the Hindu employees). If you disregard their advice, you will reach the height of fulfilment. This recluse knows of this (fulfilment) as if he is seeing it with his own eyes.[28]

5. ***To Shykh Muhammad Ashiq***

....I have received your weighty letter....

According to whatever this recluse (meaning himself) has learnt (from the occult world), Ahmad Shah Abdali will come again for putting down the enemies. When this sacred promise is fulfilled, he will most probably stay here, and dedicate his life to the last to (the welfare of) this land. In spite of the crimes that abound and the evils that have multiplied, the work is proceeding according to plan. The reason for this most probably is that Allah wants to destroy the power of his enemies.[29]

6. ***To Shah Muhammad Ashiq Pahalti***

....your letter has arrived....

Safdar Jang had reached such a state (of damnation) that his foot got afflicted with cancer. The more they removed the (affected) flesh from his foot, the worse it became. At last, they were forced to amputate his foot. Finally, he passed away in this piteous condition. It means that Allah's wrath against the Marhatahs and the Jats has now become manifest, and the defeat and destruction of these people has been decided at the occult level.[30]

7. ***To Taj Muhammad Khan Baluch***

Your honoured letter regarding suppression of the Jats has arrived. Allah is merciful, and it is hoped that he will crush the enemy. You should rest assured... You should forge unity with Musa Khan and other Muslim groups, and put to use this friendship and unity for facing the enemies. I hope for sure that on account of this unity among Muslims and their nobility, victory will be achieved. Allah says in the

---

[28] Ibid., pp.106-07.

[29] Ibid., pp.116-17.

[30] Ibid., pp.125-26. Safdar Jang had invited Shah Waliullah's holy wrath because he took help from the Marathas and the Jats in his struggle with the Sunni court faction in 1753 AD. He had been ousted from his post as Prime Minister of the Mughal emperor Ahmad Shah.

The reason for the rise of enemies and the fall of Muslims is nothing except that, led by their lower nature, Muslims have shared their (Muslims') concerns with Hindus. It is obvious that Hindus will not tolerate the suppression of non-Muslims. Being farsighted and practising patience are praiseworthy things, but not to the extent that non-Muslims take possession of Muslim cities, and go on occupying one (such) city every day... This is no time for farsightedness and patience. This is the time for putting trust in Allah, for manifesting the might of the sword, and for arousing the Muslim sense of honour. If you will do that, it is possible that winds of favour will start blowing. Whatever this recluse knows is this that war with the Jats is a magic spell which appears fearful at first but which, if you depend fully on the power of Allah and draw His attention towards this (war), will turn out to be no more than a mere show. Let me hope that you will keep me informed of developments and the faring of your arms....[31]

---

[31] Ibid., pp.150-51.

CHAPTER VII
JOURNEY FROM *JIHĀD* TO *JEE-HUZŪRĪ*

"It is obvious to your exalted self that the alien people from distant lands have become the rulers of territories and times, and the traders and vendors of goods have attained the rank of sovereignty. They have destroyed the dominions of the big grandees and the estates of the nobles of illustrious ranks, and their honour and authority have been completely set at naught... As soon as the land of Hindustan is cleared of the alien enemies and the efforts of these people [the Wahabis] result in the achievement of their objective, the ranks and offices of the state and government would be handed over to the seekers [of these], and the roots of their power and sovereignty would be strengthened."[1]

This was the message which Syed Ahmad Barelvi sent to Raja Hindu Rao, brother-in-law of Maharaja Daulat Rao Scindia (AD 1795-1827) of Gwalior.

THE DOUBLE-FACED DECEIVER

In another letter, which he wrote to his contemporary Muslim magnates ran as follows: "My real object is the establishment of *jihad* against the Sikhs of the Punjab and not to stay in the countries of Afghanistan and Yagistan. The long-haired infidels who have seized sovereignty over Punjab are very experienced, clever and deceitful... The ill-natured Sikhs and the ill-fated polytheists have gained control over the Western parts of India from the banks of Indus to the capital city of Delhi."[2]

The second letter is found in this form in *Sawānih Ahmadī,* a biography of Barelvi. But there is another version, preserved in Patna University Library, which reads as under: "My real objective is the establishment of *jihad* and carrying of war into Hindustan and not to stay in the lands of Khorasan... The Christian infidels who have gained possession over India are very artful and deceptive... The ill-natured Christians and ill-fated *Mushriks* have gained control over the various parts of India stretching from the bank of Indus to the shore of the ocean which covers a distance of six months journey."[3]

Obviously, this version was meant for the consumption of Muslim masses. It is on record that Barelvi was not only seeking monetary help

---

[1] Qeyamuddin Ahmad, *The Wahabi Movement in India,* Calcutta, 1966, pp. 365-366

[2] Ibid., p.358. He uses the term 'polytheists' for Sikhs who had not yet started swearing by monotheism, and were regarded as a Hindu sect.

[3] Ibid. This letter refers to both the British and the Sikhs who are again denounced as *mushriks*, polytheists.

from Hindu Rajas but also patronage for his followers who were operating from within India. Hindu Rajas, however, were not against the Sikhs. At the same time, he was seeking help from Muslim magnates, most of whom were against the Sikhs but allied with the British. Muslim masses alone were inimical to both. Many Muslim theologians have followed in the footsteps of the first Christian missionary, St. Paul, and tried to be 'all things to all men'. Barelvi was neither the first such Muslim missionary nor the last. But he achieved a minor miracle when he remained convinced that it was the Sikhs and the British who were clever and deceitful. Such a combination of scoundrelism and self-righteousness is rare even among Muslim theologians and missionaries.

Shri Seshadri has given a brief account of Syed Ahmad Barelvi and his Wahabis in *The Tragic Story of Partition.*[4] He has also related how Muslim leaders did a right-about-turn under the guidance of Sir Syed Ahmed Khan. We will only fill in a few more details because this episode in the history of Islam in India is extremely revealing. Marxist and Muslim scholars have been presenting the Wahabis and the Faraizis as freedom fighters and peasant revolutionaries. We should study some relevant facts in order to find out whose freedom they were fighting for, and what sort of revolution they were seeking to bring about.

ANTI-BRITISH *JIHĀD* ALWAYS ENDED AS ANTI-HINDU

We have already related in an earlier chapter how the residues of Islamic imperialism had reacted immediately after the Mughal empire collapsed in the first half of the 18th century. Shah Waliullah was a voluminous exponent of that reaction. But his appeals for an India-wide *jihād* against the Marathas had borne very little fruit. Ahmad Shah Abdali of Afghanistan, whom Waliullah had invited to join the *jihād,* inflicted a major military defeat on the Marathas in the Third Battle of Panipat in 1761 AD. But he also could not salvage the Mughal empire from the slough of disintegration into which it had sunk. By the time Waliullah was succeeded by his son Abdul Aziz (1746-1822) in the theological saddle at Delhi, the Marathas were already on the retreat before the fast advancing British. So Abdul Aziz converted his father's *jihād* against the Marathas into a *jihād* against the British. A *fatwa* was issued that India under British rule had become a *Dār-ul-harb* (zone of war or infidel land) and that it was the duty of all *mu'mins* either to migrate to a *Dār-ul-Islām* (Islamic country) or to fight the *firanghī* for

[4] Chapter 3.

the restoration of Muslim rule.

Abdul Aziz found a devoted disciple in Syed Ahmad Barelvi. To start with, he sent Barelvi to get training in the art of warfare by joining the army of Amir Khan, the Pindari chieftain. Next, he commissioned Barelvi to go to Mecca in order to acquire the requisite religions zeal. Barelvi arrived in Mecca in 1822. He travelled extensively in Arabia and Syria and met many masters of Islamic lore. It is not certain whether he met Abdul Wahab, the founder of the Wahabi Movement in Arabia. But the similarity of his ideas with those of his Arabian contemporary earned for his movement the name Wahabi, though he himself had designated it as *Tarīqah-i-Muhammadiyah* (the way of Muhammad). In any case, he came back to India towards the end of 1822 fully convinced of his mission, which was to purify Islam in India of all non-Islamic accretions and then, with the help of this revived Islam, establish an Islamic state *a la* the model prescribed by the Prophet and the first four pious Caliphs. In the process, the British were to be driven out of India by means of a *jihād*.

Barelvi was quite successful in setting up a network of centres in various cities of North India. He enlisted an impressive following, particularly among the upper class Muslims. He also collected a lot of money at the same time. He called upon Muslims to eliminate three kinds of excesses — firstly, those advocated by heterodox Sufis; secondly, those practised by the Shias; and thirdly, those 'borrowed' from the Hindus. Prof. Aziz Ahmad writes: "This last category was by far the most important, and was most vigorously denounced by Sayyid Ahmad Barelvi. It had included pilgrimage to Hindu holy places, shouting Hindu religious slogans, and adorning the tombs with *lingams* (Hindu phallic symbol), worship of Hindu deities, borrowing from Hindu animism, consulting Brahmins for good or bad omens, and celebration of Hindu festivals. Next came external Hindu manners, such as eating on leaves or keeping pig-tails or piercing women's ears and nose to wear jewellery or shaving one's hair and eyebrows in imitation of *yogis* or even dressing like Hindus."[5]

Barelvi forgot that a majority of Muslims in India were converts from the Hindu fold, and that Islam sat rather lightly on most of them. This is understandable. After all, Barelvi was an Islamic missionary and not a historian of Islam in India. What amazes one is that even Muslim scholars in modern times have managed to forget that the 'impurities' or 'excesses' of Islam in India were not injected into it by Hindus from the outside, but were brought along by Hindu converts

[5] Aziz Ahmad, *Studies in Islamic Culture*, Pp. 211-212.

who were driven or lured into the fold of Islam by force or fraud. Nor has any Muslim scholar noted that it is these 'impurities' and 'excesses' which have prevented the total brutalization of native Muslims such as had always been and is being advocated by their *Ashrāf* (foreign) mentors.

To resume the story, Barelvi's confidence in a *jihād* against the British collapsed when he surveyed the extent and the magnitude of British power in India. He did the next best under the circumstances, and declared a *jihād* against the Sikh power in the Punjab, Kashmir and the North-West Frontier. The British on their part welcomed this change and permitted Barelvi to travel towards the border of Afghanistan at a leisurely pace, collecting money and manpower along the way. It was during this journey that Barelvi stayed with or met several Hindu princes, feigned that his fulminations against the Sikhs were a fake, and that he was going out of India in order to establish a base for fighting against the British. It is surmised that some Hindu princes took him at his word, and gave him financial help. To the Muslim princes, however, he told the truth, namely, that he was up against the Sikhs because they "do not allow the call to prayer from mosques and the killing of cows"[6]

Barelvi set up his base in the North-West Frontier near Afghanistan. The active assistance he expected from the Afghan king did not materialise because that country was in a mess at that time. But the British connived at the constant flow not only of a sizable manpower but also of a lot of finance. Muslim magnates in India were helping him to the hilt. His basic strategy was to conquer Kashmir before launching his major offensive against the Punjab. But he met with very little success in that direction in spite of several attempts. Finally, he met his Waterloo in 1831 when the Sikhs under Kunwar Sher Singh stormed his citadel at Balakot. The great *mujāhid* fell in the very first battle he ever fought. His corpse along with that of his second in command was burnt, and the ashes were scattered in the winds. Muslims hail him as a *shahīd*.

[6] *Targhīb-al-Jīhād* translated by W.W. Hunter, p.140. The fond belief that the Amir of Afghanistan and the Frontier Tribals could be invited for liberating India from foreign rule, lingered for a long time. It was soon forgotten that the belief was entertained or fostered by Muslim 'revivalists' in the 18th and the 19th centuries. The Indian "revolutionaries" like M.N. Roy, Raja Mahendra Pratap, and Chandrashekhar Azad were latter-day victims of this illusion and tried to help 'our friends in the North-West' with munitions and money. The illusion suffered a set back only when Pandit Nehru went out to the NWF to fraternize with the 'brave Pathans' soon after becoming virtual Prime Minister of India in 1946, and was welcomed with bullets. He never mentioned the 'brave Pathans' again.

The scattered remnants of the Wahabis fought a few more skirmishes with the Sikhs. But they also met with no success. Next, they turned their fury against the British when the latter took over from the Sikhs in 1849. There was a lot of organizing and shouting of *Allah-o-Akbar* in the North-West Frontier as well as in several centres inside India such as Patna, Meerut, Bareilly and Hyderabad. But they produced very little fight. The British smashed them everywhere and it was all over by 1870. The greatest 'achievement' of the Wahabis after four decades of 'fighting' was the murder of Justice Norman at Calcutta in 1871, and of Lord Mayo, the Viceroy, at Port Blair in 1872.

One of Barelvi's distinguished disciples was Mir Nasser Ali of Barasat in Bengal, better known as Titu Mir or Titu Mian. He had met the master in Mecca in 1822, and returned to Calcutta a few years later in order to organize another *jihād* against the British. He set up his headquarters at Barasat, and declared that India under British rule was a *Dār-ul-harb*. But, in due course, his invectives also came to be increasingly directed against the unarmed Hindus in the countryside of Bengal.

Narahari Kaviraj, a Communist scholar who hails Titu's rascals as peasant revolutionaries, describes the exploits of his hero in the following words: "They first sallied forth in a body of about 500 persons to attack the market place of the village known as Poorwa, where they slaughtered a cow. With the blood of the animal they defiled a Hindu temple. Then they hung up the four quarters (of the cow) in the different parts of the market place. They maltreated and wounded an unfortunate Brahmin and threatened to make him a Muslim... The village of Laoghatty in the Nadia district was their next object attack. Here they commenced operations by the repetition of the same outrage to the religious feelings of the Hindus which they had committed at Poorwa, viz, the slaughter of a cow in that part of the village exclusively occupied by Hindu residents. But being opposed by Hardeb Ray, a principal inhabitant of the village, and a Brahmin, at the head of a party of villagers, an affray ensued in which one Debnath Ray was killed and Hardeb Ray and a number of villagers were severely wounded... Titu's party went on increasing and with growing confidence they went on killing cows in different places, making raids on the neighbouring villages, forcing from the raiyats agreements to furnish grain, compelling many of them to profess conformity to the tenets of their sect... They openly proclaimed themselves masters of the country, asserting that the Mussalmans from whom the English usurped it, were the rightful owners of the empire... The rebels issued parwanas to the principal zamindars of the district. Their tenor was as follows: 'This country is now given to our *Deen Mohammed.* You must, therefore, immediately send grain to the army.' In a written report the magistrate of Nadia states that a paper written in Bengali and signed in Arabic characters, was put into his hand, purporting to be an order of Allah to the Pal Chowdhuries of Ranaghat to supply *russud* (rations) to the army of fakirs who were about to fight with the government."[7] All of this was an early rehearsal of what the Moplahs were to do in Malabar in 1921 during the Khilafat agitation against the British.

The British government at Calcutta had to take action at last, not because it was bothered about what was happening to the Hindus at the hands of Muslim *mujāhids* but because the Wahabis of Bengal were becoming a menace to the British system of law and order. Titu Mian was killed in the very first encounter with a British battalion in 1839. A number of his followers were hanged or sentenced to various terms of imprisonment.

Another movement on similar lines had flared up simultaneously in the Faridpur district of Bengal. This was the Faraizi Movement launched by Shariatullah who also had spent 20 years in Mecca and Medina. He had also declared that India under the British was a *Dār-ul-harb,* and that Muslims should not observe Friday prayers and the two *Ids* till Islamic rule was restored. He also tried to 'purify' Islam of 'un-Islamic accretions' borrowed from the hated Hindus. And he also acquired a large following of fanatic Muslims in order to mount his *jihād* against the British. But like his contemporary, Titu Mian, he also ended by spending all his spleen against the Hindus. Kaviraj writes: "As the followers of Shariatullah increased in numbers, and as they became too bold and overbearing, they carried their incursions against Hindu zamindars and committed acts of cruelty against Hindu families."[8] Shariatullah died in 1837 without achieving anything more spectacular. That was left to his son who had meanwhile returned from Mecca after a stay of several years.

Muhammad Mohsin, better known as Dudhu Mian (1819-1860), was a more full-fledged fundamentalist than his father. Professor Murray Titus writes that "Among other things, we are told that he insisted upon his disciples eating the common grass-hopper *(phaḍinga)*, which they detested, because the locust *(tiḍḍi)* was used as food in Arabia."[9] Dudhu Mian was convinced that Allah had entrusted him with the mission of restoring Islam in India to its pristine purity and

[7] Narahari Kaviraj, *Wahabi And Faraizi Rebels of Bengal,* New Delhi, 1982, Pp.37-38, 43-44, 50-51.

[8] Ibid., p.65.

[9] Murray Titus, *Indian Islam,* Oxford, 1930, p.180.

bygone glory. That implied a fight against the British. But like his father, he also found that the unarmed Hindus in the countryside of Bengal were a far more attractive prey. According to Kaviraj, Dudhu's followers were well-armed with swords, shields and a variety of other weapons. In April 1839, they raided 76 Hindu houses in seven villages. They committed atrocities on innocent Hindus, killed cows and broke the images worshipped by the Brahmins inside their homes. Later on, one of their victims was Kalicharan Kanjilal, a gomashta in a British-owned Indigo factory. Kanjilal was given the full treatment prescribed for *kāfirs* in the Quran and the Sunnah of the Prophet. The atrocities heaped on this poor and unoffending Hindu by a Islamic-cum-Communist 'hero' are described in detail in contemporary government records.

Finally, the British Indigo planters put pressure on the British government to bring the hoodlum to book. "He was charged with plunder in 1838, committed to sessions for murder in 1841, tried for trespass and for unlawful assembly in 1844, and for abduction and plunder in 1846. But it was found impossible to induce witnesses to give evidence, and on each occasion he was acquitted."[10] It was only in 1857 that he was put in jail without trial. He died there in 1860.

The last effort made by the *mujāhids* of all sorts to overthrow the British rule and restore the 'Muslim empire in India' was in 1857. They were able to enlist Hindu support on a large scale because of reasons in which we need not go here. But this grand *jihād* was also defeated, and its leaders had to seek shelter in the Hindu kingdom of Nepal. The last Mughal emperor ended his days of disgrace in far off Rangoon. Ishtiq Husain Qureshi names this period as that of the 'lowest depths of broken pride'.[11]

Thus, by about the year 1860, the multifarious *mujāhids* had emptied themselves of all the heat stored in them by their sojourn in the 'holy land' of Hijaz. They could not shake a single brick in the edifice of the British empire. It was now the turn of the Muslim magnates, sitting pretty in their palatial mansions, to rescue the *mujāhids* from the theological knots into which the latter had tied themselves. Meanwhile, the British had seen the Muslim potential for mischief against the Hindus who had started taking pride in their history and heritage, and demanding self-rule. An invitation was extended to the residues of Islamic imperialism to revise their strategy when W.W. Hunter wrote

---

[10] R.C. Majumdar (ed.), *History and Culture of the Indian People*, Volume XI, Bombay, 1981, p.885.

[11] Ihtiaq Husain Qureshi, *The Muslim Community of the Indo-Pakistan Subcontinent* (610-1947), Delhi reprint, 1985, Chapter XI.

The Indian Musalmans in 1871. The invitation was readily accepted by the other side.

ISLAMIC THEOLOGIANS DO A RIGHT-ABOUT TURN

Shri Seshadri has referred to this part of the story. He writes: "It was the vested landed interests amongst the Muslim aristocracy, especially in Oudh and parts of U.P. and Bihar which succeeded in persuading the maulvis to issue *fatwas* with a view to contradicting the previous *fatwas* calling for the establishment of *Darul-Islam*. The *fatwas* issued by the heads of the three prominent Mussalman sects of Mecca declared that the Mussalmans under the Christian rule of the British were assured of protection and liberty of Islamic observances and as such it was not *Darul-harb* and did not warrant jehad against it."[12] The mullahs in Mecca had been 'persuaded' by the British to help the Muslims in India.

Thus what had started with a bang ended with a whimper. The Mullahs have always had a hundred tricks in their theological hat. They can turn into white to-day what they had pronounced black only a day before, and vice versa. Hunter had noted in his book that "The danger to British rule comes from the 'fanatic masses', who take their religion seriously unlike the 'well-to-do Musalmans' who contrive to evade the clear prescriptions of the Quran to flee or to rebel".[13]

It was at this critical juncture in the history of Islam in India that Sir Syed Ahmed stepped forward. "He was a pupil of the famous Mawlānā a Mamlūk 'Ali who was entirely a product of the Walī-u'llahī school and tradition. It was perhaps because of this relationship that he claimed to be a Wahhābī..."[14] But now on the word 'Wahabi' was to acquire a new meaning. He had been a protege of the British for a long time. He had sided with his masters during the *jihād* of 1857. Soon after the *jihād* failed, he came out with a book, *The Loyal Mohammedans of India*. He travelled to England in 1869 and wrote as follows from there to a friend in India: "Without flattering the English, I can truly say that the natives of India, high and low, merchants and petty shopkeepers, educated and illiterate, when contrasted with the English in education, manners and uprightness, are as like them as a dirty animal is to an able and handsome man. Do you look upon an animal as a thing to be honoured? Do you think it necessary to treat an animal courteously, or the reverse? We have no right to courteous treatment.

---

[12] *The Tragic Story of Partition*, p.65.

[13] Cited by David Lelyveld, *Aligarh's First Generation*, Princeton, 1978, p.11.

[14] Ishtiq Husain Qureshi, *Ulema in Politics*, Delhi reprint, p.226.

The English have reason for believing us in India to be imbecile brutes."[15]

Here was the man the British were looking for. The rest of his role is too well-known to be repeated here. He was undoubtedly the father of the two-nation theory which led later on to the demand for Pakistan. He became a bitter opponent of the Indian National Congress as soon as it was founded in 1885. He decried parliamentary democracy as a plot to put the 'brute Hindu majority' into power. He led a hate campaign against the Bengalis who were in the forefront of the fight for freedom. He was all for a fight against Hindi attaining an equal status with Urdu. And he tried his best to build bridges between Christianity on the one hand and Islam on the other. The nett result of his Aligarh Movement was to convert the Muslim community into a close preserve of toadyism *(jee-huzūrī)* towards the British. The British on their part responded positively, and made many concessions to the Muslims. This co-operation between British imperialism and the residues of Islamic imperialism continued till the creation of Pakistan, except for a brief period of bad blood during the Khilafat agitation.

Many scholars, both Hindu and Muslim, have persisted in painting Sir Syed as a nationalist in his early career. They feel puzzled at what they call his sudden volte face. The earliest of these scholars was Lala Lajpat Rai. Lalaji's father had become a Muslim for all practical purposes, and was a great admirer of Sir Syed. The son had also come under the same influence before he went to Lahore and joined the Arya Samaj. He became an ardent nationalist. But the favourable impression which Sir Syed had made on his mind earlier had lingered on. He was, therefore, shocked when Sir Syed appeared in what Lalaji thought to be a new attire. He wrote a number of Open Letters to Sir Syed which were published in the English and the Varnacular press of his days. These letters made Lalaji famous in no time, and all over India.

Shri Seshadri has also observed that "these nationalist ideas appear to be but a fleeting phase in Sir Syed's life". The truth, however, is that there was never a nationalist phase in the life of Sir Syed. He started his life as a lick-spittle of the British, and a lick-spittle he remained to the end of his days. But like his namesake of earlier days, Syed Ahmad Barelvi, he tried to humour the Hindus whenever he needed material help. M.R.A. Baig hits the nail on the head when he writes: "As is well-known, he secured donations for Aligarh from Hindus of his own feudal class. When canvassing for their support he expressed such exem-

[15] Cited by G.F.L. Graham, *Sir Syed Ahmad Khan*, London, 1885, Pp.183-184.

plary sentiments as that Hindus and Muslims were the 'two eyes of the beautiful Indian bride.' But when addressing exclusively Muslim audiences, especially political meetings, he was militant enough to threaten civil war."[16]

Five years after Sir Syed's death in 1898, his successor, Viqar-ul-Mulk, wrote a letter to *The Pioneer* of Lucknow. He said: "We start with the firm conviction and seek to implant it in the mind of every Indian Musalman that our destiny is now bound up with the presence and permanence of British rule in this country, and that in the government of the day we have got our best and surest friend."[17]

This was the mentality which led to the formation of the Muslim League in December, 1906. The League pledged itself to an ever-lasting loyalty to the British Crown. Three months later, Viqar-ul-Mulk addressed a students' gathering at Aligarh. He said: "God forbid, if the British rule disappears from India. Hindus will lord over it, and we will be in constant danger of our life, property and honour. The only way for the Muslims to escape this danger is to help in the continuance of the British rule. If the Muslims are heartily with the British, then that rule is bound to endure. Let the Muslims consider themselves as a British army ready to shed their blood and sacrifice their lives for the British Crown... Wherever you are, whether in the football field or in the tennis lawn, you have to consider yourselves as soldiers of a British regiment. You have to defend the British Empire, and to give the enemy [Hindus] a fight in doing so. If you bear it in mind and act accordingly, you will have done that and your name will be written in letters of gold in the British Indian history. The future generations will be grateful to you."[18]

But the leaders of the Indian National Congress continued to hug the illusion that the residues of Islamic imperialism in India could also be mobilised in the fight for the freedom of the motherland. They had failed to notice and understand why the *jihād* against the British had again and again led to atrocities on innocent Hindus, and how the *mujāhids* of yester years had ended by becoming stooges of the British at a later stage.

---

[16] M.R.A. Baig, *The Muslim Dilemma in India,* Delhi, 1974, p.52.

[17] Francis Robinson, *Separatism Among Indian Muslims,* Delhi, 1975, p.139.

[18] Cited by R.C. Majumdar (ed.), *History and Culture of the Indian People,* Volume XI, Bombay,1981, p.146.

Chapter VIII
NATIONAL RESURGENCE REVILED AS HINDU REVIVALISM

Maharshi Dayananda Saraswati (1824-1883) was speaking at a meeting in Calcutta when some stones were thrown at him by some members of the audience disgruntled by his criticism of Hindu orthodoxy. He remained calm and self-possessed. He appealed for a patient hearing in the following words: "The British Government has guaranteed freedom of speech to all of us. Why should I be deprived of that freedom? Please! Let me say what I want to say. Those who disagree with me will also have their turn."

This part of his speech was reported to the then Viceroy of India. The Viceroy thought that the Maharshi was a great well-wisher of the British Raj. The Maharshi was, therefore, invited to the Government House and given a warm reception by the Viceroy himself. An official interpreter was standing close by to establish communication between the Indian recluse and the representative of the mightiest empire in world history.

After a brief spell of some small talk, the Viceroy broached the subject he had on his mind. He said: "Swami, the people of India have started forgetting the benefits conferred on them by the British Raj. They are being misled by some mischief-makers. You did well to remind the people of Calcutta that it was the Raj which had given them freedom of speech. I hope you will keep on telling the same truth to your countrymen everywhere you go. Freedom of speech is not the only benefit we have brought to India. There are many more. I am sure you known them all."

The Maharshi found it difficult to hide his embarrassment. He kept quiet and looked away. The Viceroy was puzzled and prodded him for an affirmation. The Maharshi had to break his silence. He said: "Sahebji, I am sorry I have been misunderstood. Forgive me for what I am being forced to say. The reference to freedom of speech was made by me in a specific context. It was not at all my intention to uphold the British usurpation of my country. Make no mistake. I consider the British Raj to be a curse. I stand for *svarājya*."

The Viceroy was taken aback as the message of the Maharshi was conveyed to him. He walked away in a huff, without so much as saying a good-bye to his great guest. The rest of the viceregal retinue melted away in the next few moments. The Maharshi walked out of the Government House, alone but unrepentant. His gait was akin to that of a lion who had dared a dangerous adversary in the latter's own den.

MESSAGE OF MAHARSHI DAYANANDA

Maharshi Dayananda lived to found the Arya Samaj in 1875. It made a great contribution to India's fight for freedom. But before the veterans of the Samaj joined the political battle, they fought for a deeper freedom of the spirit. That was the message of the Maharshi—the surrenders made by our people at the spiritual, cultural, psychological and ideological levels had to go before the shackles at the physical level could be broken.

During the days of Muslim military domination, some sections of the national elite in some parts of the country had started kowtowing to the imperialist ideology and totalitarian culture of Islam. The same or some other collaborationist sections had been similarly cowed down by the imperialist ideology and culture of Christianity, soon after the British succeeded in seizing political power by force of arms. The twin surrenders were joining forces and working havoc with the morale of our people when the Maharshi appeared on the scene.

The Maharshi was the first great Indian in modern times to see through both Islam and Christianity. He challenged the claims of these closed theologies masquerading as religion. And he appealed to his people to eschew every element which Indian culture had borrowed or imbibed from these alien cultures. He called Islamic and Christian cultures alien not because they had come from foreign lands but because they were contrary to the basic canons of rationalism, universalism and humanism, enshrined in the ancient Indian culture.

But that was the least significant part of the Maharshi's message. He made a positive contribution when he pointed out that India had inherited a spirituality and a culture which were not only indigenous but also intrinsically superior to the imported creeds and cultures. He encouraged and enabled his people to reawaken to their own inner sources of strength, and hold their heads high in the face of foreign invaders. He was the first to use the terms *swadeshī* and *swarājya.*

At the same time, the Maharshi restored the Veda to its rightful place as the permanent and profound centre of Indian spirituality, culture and social philosophy. His people had lost consciousness of this centre when they had started drawing a sharp line between *nishreyasa* (highest good) and *abhyudaya* (worldly welfare), between here and hereafter, between spirituality and science. They had become dwarfed in mind and emaciated in body because, to start with, they had separated these two from their unity in the Spirit.

He did something more. He raised an accusing finger against the heavy weight of empty rituals and outmoded social traditions which were smothering India's indigenous society. There was a meaningless multiplication of sects and cults. Superstition and magic had replaced religion in many cases. Education had been reduced to a matter of cramming certain traditional texts. Health had been ruined by early marriages, and the lack of a proper physical culture. Women had been driven into *purdah,* and deprived of their proper status as equal partners with men in all spheres of life. And a sizable section of our society had been condemned to live as untouchables, without an opportunity to make their own characteristic contributions to social welfare. The Maharshi appealed to his people to throw away all this dead wood, and start breathing again in the unpolluted air of that spirituality and science for which India had been famous in ages past.

BANKIM CHANDRA CHATTERJEE

A younger contemporary of Maharshi Dayananda had meanwhile dived deep into the ocean of Indian culture and come up with a vast and variegated treasure. That was Bankim Chandra Chatterjee (1838-1894). The Maharshi had never known what was passing for modern education and his know-ledge of the West as well as of Christianity had perforce to be second-hand. Bankim Chandra did not suffer from this disadvantage. He acquired a wide knowledge of Western philosophy, sociology and science from the horse's mouth. He also knew Christianity from its original sources. He was thus placed in a good position to compare his own heritage with whatever was being trumpeted about as the latest and the best from the West.

Bankim Chandra brought out the shallowness of modern Indology in two short satirical essays. The poverty of mind at the back of Western scholarship vis-a-vis Hinduism was thus brilliantly portrayed. He also questioned the notion current in his times that India had always been a game for every foreign invader. It was he who showed with facts and dates and for the first time that the Islamic sword which had swept so swiftly over a large part of the world had taken a long time even to breach the borders of India, and that it had failed in the final round. Our people were thus enabled to look back at their past with a sense of pride.

It was also Bankim Chandra who restored the Mahabharata to its rightful place as a profound elaboration of what the Veda had said in the form of mystic *mantras.* The Gita which had been subjected to sectarian interpretations for several centuries past, was rescued by

Bankim Chandra from the quagmire of casuistry. This great scripture had been interpreted by many *āchāryas* either to support *sannyāsa* or to bolster *bhakti*. Its central core of *karmayoga* had been consigned to oblivion. Bankim Chandra was the first in modern times to restore the lost balance, so much so that in his *Ānandamaṭha* it was the *sannyāsin* who took up the sword in defence of Dharma. In days to come, the Gita was to become the greatest single inspiration for revolutionary action. Many a freedom fighter mounted the gallows with the Gita in his hands and Bankim Chandra's *Vande Mātaram* on his lips.

But the greatest achievement of Bankim Chandra was the rehabilitation of Sri Krishna of the Mahabharata. This highest Hindu image of the seer, the statesman, and the hero had been made to sing and dance with the *gopīs* for far too long. Some devotees of Sri Krishna's dalliance with the *gopīs* had gone to the extent of saying that Krishna had ceased to be Krishna as soon as he left Vrindavana. Bankim Chandra did not fall foul of this portrayal. Instead, he quietly brought back the Krishna who had sided with the just cause in a controversy involving Dharma, who had befriended Draupadi in moments of her great distress, who had guided the Pandavas through every twist and turn of fortune, who had given the Gita on the battlefield of Kurukshetra, who had rescued Yudhisthira from a fit of unmanly remorse, but who had nonetheless bowed before Bhishma as that paragon of valour, virtue, and wisdom lay on his deathbed.

SWAMI VIVEKANANDA

Soon after Bankim Chandra, another brilliant star rose on the spiritual horizon of Bharatavarsha. That was Swami Vivekananda (1863-1902). He was a great *shishya* of a great *guru*. He started as a spiritual seeker. But such was the sweep of his vision that it soon embraced every type of human suffering in the world. The plight of his own countrymen invited his particular attention. He started with the Upanishadic message, *uttiṣṭha, jāgrata varān nibodhah*. But such was the depth of his sympathy for the poor and the downtrodden that in reply to a question by one of his disciples, he said: "The poor, the ignorant, the illiterate, the afflicted, let these be your God; know that service to these is the highest religion." He warned his people that they had mistaken their *tamas* (inertia) for *adhyātma* (spirituality), and that it was a fatal folly.

Vivekananda was the first Indian to see clearly that Christianity had no intrinsic worth, and that the missionaries in India were making inroads into Hindu society simply because they were equipped with huge financial resources supplied by Western countries. He was also the first to carry a campaign against Christian imperialism into the latter's own homeland. At the same time, he made India's universal spirituality known to the world. Here was a genuine spirituality, he said, which was not at all in conflict with modern science, unlike the theology of Christianity which had recoiled at the very first touch of the scientific temper. Thus he had placed himself truly in the tradition of those monks and mystics who had carried the message of India's universal spirituality to many foreign lands, before Christian and Islamic imperialism had raised an impenetrable wall in their way.

It was only a few years after the passing away of Swami Vivekananda that the world witnessed what Shri H.V. Seshadri has described as 'A Nation Bestirred' in *The Tragic Story of Partition.* The stir had frightened the British rulers as well as the residues of Islamic imperialism — the descendants of foreign swordsmen and Sufis who had brought the terrorist creed of Islam to this country .

Not many people remember it now that before the Partition in 1947, there had been another Partition, almost along the same lines and brought about by a combination of the same forces. That was the Partition of Bengal in 1905 which gave a brute majority to the Muslims in the very heartland of India's national resurgence. Shri Seshadri has devoted a whole chapter to it in his book. He quotes *The Statesman* of Calcutta which had stated editorially that the Partition of Bengal was intended "to foster in Eastern Bengal the growth of Mohammedan power which, it is hoped, will have the effect of keeping in check the rapidly growing strength of the Hindu community."[1]

This first Partition had to be annulled because an awakened nation offered a stiff resistance. The national vision had not yet become vitiated by an obsessive pre-occupation with the so-called communal problem. It was this National Vision which nurtured programmes like Swadeshi, boycott, and non-cooperation. It could also see clearly that the British rule was based on brute force, and that the nation had a right to use force for the overthrow of that rule .

SRI AUROBINDO

The Partition of Bengal converted Bankim Chandra's *Vande Mātaram* into a *mantra* by reciting which our people scaled the highest heights of courage and sacrifice. But what made that brief episode important in the history of our fight for freedom was the emergence of

[1] *The Tragic Story of Partition,* p. 30.

another great seer and sage. That was Sri Aurobindo (1872-1950). He shot like a meteor across the political sky, and soon retired into a self-chosen seclusion in search of new visions and victories. But the trail he blazed in the realm of India's spirituality and culture yet holds the promise of a still more dazzling dawn.

Sri Aurobindo confirmed and completed the ideological work undertaken by his predecessors — Maharshi Dayananda, Bankim Chandra and Swami Vivekananda. The National Vision now became a vision which had fully awakened to *Sanātana Dharma* in all its dimensions. It was the ancient Vedic Vision at its highest and best. Sri Aurobindo's insights into India's inheritance — spiritual, philosophical, cultural, artistic, social, and political — went very far in restoring our people's legitimate pride in their great past. He was very soon hailed as the Prophet of Indian Nationalism.

THE NATIONAL VISION GETS VITIATED

But, unfortunately, there were several other forces simmering below the surface. Several generations of Hindus had by now been fed upon Western education based on a materialist world-view, evolutionistic sociology, utilitarian ethics, hedonistic psychology and parliamentary politics. They had also swallowed heavy doses of Christianity disguised as Comparative Religion. And what was worst of all, they had become addicted to the Western version of Indian history and culture.

These self-alienated people behaved exactly as had been anticipated by Macaulay and his cohorts who had laid the foundations of a new educational system on the ruins of an old network which had moulded the national mind for ages untold. Their highest spiritual value was a mechanical monotheism, and a way of worship borrowed from the Christian Church. Their highest cultural aspiration was to dress, dine, dance, and decorate their drawing rooms after the fashion of their British masters, Their highest social aspiration was a self-centred and acquisitive individualism which frowned at every facet of the traditional social system. And their highest political aspiration was a Dominion Status within the British Empire.

Some of the leaders thrown up by this class of Indians were men of unimpeachable character. Shri Seshadri has paid handsome tributes to them for their "qualities of head and heart". But, at the same time, he has noted that they could not rise above the limitations imposed upon them by their education and training. They could not think of India as a great and ancient nation which had suffered a decline as a result of imperialist inroads, Islamic and British. To them, India was still a "nation in the making".

THE TERMINOLOGICAL SWINDLE

Meanwhile, Hindu society had been reduced from the status of a nation to that of a religious community in the counting of heads which the British rulers described as their census operation. Nationalism was now increasingly being labelled as Hindu Communalism. A revaluation of the national resurgence could not lag far behind. It was soon stigmatised as Hindu Revivalism. This new terminology which was being used by a growing tribe of sociologists and political scientists had far-reaching ideological implications.

On the other hand, Islam was getting raised from the status of an imperialist ideology to that of a religion. The residues of Islamic imperialism were now being rehabilitated as the representatives of a religious community which was in a 'minority' and which was trying to 'save' itself from the 'domination of a majority'. The frantic efforts of a foreign fraternity to retain its unequal rights and privileges, earned during the days of its military domination, were now being described as 'a minority's struggle for self-identity'. At the same time, Islamic Atavism and resultant Muslim Separatism were being renamed as Muslim Revivalism. Here, too, the use of a new terminology had far-reaching ideological consequences.

This terminological swindle took place at the turn of the 19th century, and was brought about by the combined efforts of the British imperialists and the residues of Islamic imperialism. They shared a problem in common. The problem was the rising tide of National Resurgence in the indigenous Hindu society. The British imperialists now started pointing out that while they 'appreciated the legitimate aspirations' of the 'majority community', they could not leave the 'minority community' at the 'mercy' of the former. The 'minority' on its part started protesting that parliamentary institutions were not at all suited to the 'peculiar conditions' of a country divided into 'rival communities', and that the Muslims could not look with equanimity at the prospect of the British leaving India till the 'majority community' had succeeded in 'winning the trust' of the 'minority community'.

THE BLIND ALLEY

The leaders of the Indian National Congress could think only in terms of a parliamentary constitution patterned on the British model. They could, therefore, see no alternative to 'winning the trust of the minority community'. That was the starting point of an endless exercise for finding a constitutional formula which could 'satisfy' the Muslims. They could not see that they were thus getting into a blind alley from which there was no way out. The reservations and weightages which the 'minority community' demanded in all spheres of national life, at every conference table, went on multiplying in direct proportion to the concessions made by the 'majority community'. And the British were always there to compete with the Nationalists in making greater and greater concessions to the Muslims.

The constitutional settlement, however, was not the only settlement which the 'minority community' was seeking. It was also objecting to every manifestation of National Culture in the public life of the country. If the Hindus sang *Vande Mātaram* in a public meeting, it was a 'conspiracy' to convert Muslims into *kāfirs*. If the Hindus blew a conch, or broke a coconut, or garlanded the portrait of a revered patriot, it was an attempt to 'force' Muslims into 'idolatry'. If the Hindus spoke in any of their native languages, it was an 'affront' to the culture of Islam. If the Hindus took pride in their pre-Islamic heroes, it was a 'devaluation' of Islamic history. And so on, there were many more objections, major and minor, to every national self-expression. In short, it was a demand that Hindus should cease to be Hindus and become instead a faceless conglomeration of rootless individuals.

On the other hand, the 'minority community' was not prepared to make the slightest concession in what they regarded as their religious and cultural rights. If the Hindus requested that cow-killing should stop, it was a demand for renouncing an 'established Islamic practice'. If the Hindus objected to an open sale of beef in the bazars, it was an 'encroachment' on the 'civil rights' of the Muslims. If the Hindus demanded that cows meant for ritual slaughter should not be decorated and marched through Hindu localities, it was 'trampling upon time-honoured Islamic traditions'. If the Hindus appealed that Hindu religious processions passing through a public thoroughfare should not be obstructed, it was an attempt to 'disturb the peace of Muslim prayers'. If the Hindus wanted their native languages to attain an equal status with Urdu in the courts and the administration, it was an 'assault on Muslim culture'. If the Hindus taught to their children the true history of Muslim tyrants, it was a 'hate campaign against Islamic heroes'. And the 'minority community' was always ready to 'defend' its 'religion and culture' by taking recourse to street riots.

THE TRANSVALUATION OF VALUES

In the process, the residues of a bygone imperialism became equal partners in staking their claims to the fruits of freedom for which they were not prepared make the slightest sacrifice In the process, traitors who were prepared to barter away India's freedom for the sake of Turkey or Saudi Arabia or some other Islamic country, started swaggering around as more than equal to the proven patriots. In the process, quislings who were sending 'invitations' to the Amir of Afghanistan or the Shah of Iran to invade India, became 'revolutionaries' whose 'idealism' could not be questioned. In short, there was a complete transvaluation of values so that the black started looking white and vice versa.

The process is still continuing in the truncated homeland which the nation has been able to retain for itself for the time being. In fact, the process is fast moving towards a climax. The residues of Islamic imperialism have not had to pay any price for their treachery and treason; on the contrary, they have attained a higher status as the 'guardians' of democracy and secularism, which in their opinion are 'being threatened by Hindu communalism, Hindu revivalism and Hindu chauvinism'. They have been joined by a motley crowd of secularists, socialists and communists, all of whom have mortgaged their minds to one imported ideology or the other. And Hindu society which constitutes the nation has been driven into a corner. Hindu leaders have been made to cry that they are not communalists, that they have renounced revivalism, that they cherish Islam as a great religion, that they regard Islamic heroes as their own heroes, that they have no use for people who regard the prevalent mode of secularism as perverse, and that they are fed up with that 'lunatic fringe' which still continues to take pride in the national heritage.

THE ONLY WAY OUT

The nation will never be able to get out of this tight corner till it clears up the terminological confusion, stops making use of meaningless words like communalism and revivalism, and rewrites its books of history, politics, and sociology in an exact and appropriate language. This exact language will substitute Nationalism for Hindu Communalism, National Resurgence for Hindu Revivalism, Islamic Atavism for Muslim Revivalism, and Islamic Imperialism for Muslim Communalism. Then alone the various elements and forces struggling for supremacy in the country at present will fall into their proper places, and come out in their true colours.

Chapter IX
LOSS OF PRIVILEGES PORTRAYED AS PRIVATION

A British scholar and civil servant, W.W. Hunter, wrote the book, *The Indian Musalmans: Are They Bound in Conscience to Rebel against the Queen?*, which was published in 1871. It was reviewed by Alfred Lyall who was soon to succeed as the Lieutenant Governor of the North West Province (later on known as U.P.). Lyall had warned that "what Hunter had said will be overheard by Indian Muslims; they will be encouraged to think of themselves as 'an oppressed people or a persecuted sect'."[1]

The warning was only a thin veneer. What Hunter had written was meant to be 'overheard' by the 'Indian' Muslims. His book had been written at the instance of Lord Mayo, the then Viceroy of India. It was intended to make it easy for the residues of Islamic imperialism to revise their stance vis-a-vis British imperialism without loss of face.

THE NEW POSTURE OF ISLAMIC IMPERIALISM

The residues of Islamic imperialism were themselves in search of a new posture which they could adopt in an adverse situation. The heroic mask which they had donned earlier as Wahabis and Faraizis had paid no dividends. The mask had been torn off their faces by the Sikh sword and the British bayonet. The only 'achievement' they could claim was the killing of some Hindu *kāfirs*, the slaughter of some cows, and the desecration of some Hindu temples in the countryside of Bengal. At the end of it all, they had nothing better to do than sit back in a mood of self-pity, and lick their wounds at leisure.

The tip given by Hunter, therefore, came in handy and at the right time. It was not long before the residues of Islamic imperialism started dropping their mask of *mujāhids,* and donning the mask of martyrs. Ever since, they have been parading themselves as a 'poor and persecuted minority'.

Hunter's tip has also stood the test of time. Generation after generation of Hindus, particularly Hindu intellectuals, have been blackmailed by this sob-story about Muslim backwardness and poverty. In fact, the sob-story has succeeded so well with the Hindus that the Muslims themselves have come to believe in it. In the process, they have carved out two separate states where they rule the roost, and from where Hindus have been either hounded out or reduced to the status of

[1] Cited by David Lelyveld, op.cit., pp. 11-12.

non-citizens. They are now reaching out to repeat the trick in what remains of the ancient Hindu homeland.

We will deal with the ballyhoo about Muslim backwardness and poverty in a subsequent chapter. Right now we want to take a peep behind the mask of martyrdom in order to see the real face that has been secreted for quite some time. That will take us back to the last quarter of the 19th century when the residues of Islamic imperialism in U.P. first started soliciting pity and sympathy for their "sorrowful plight".

MUSLIMS INSIST ON COW-SLAUGHTER

The opening wail of woe was heard when Hindus in U.P. decided to call a halt to the open sale of beef in the bazars. Hindus had been helpless in the matter of cow-slaughter so long as Muslims were at the centre of power. Hindus were helpless even now about the British slaughtering of cows in many military cantonments. But they thought that they could do something about it in those towns where they were in a majority in the newly constituted municipalities. So they started adopting resolutions for a ban on open sale of beef in the bazars, and for moving the slaughter-houses out of city precincts.

The Muslim response was not merely recalcitrant; it was positively hostile. The Mullahs came out with *fatwas* that Id festivities could not be completed without sacrificing cows. Muslim scholars pronounced that the 'prosperous' Hindus were trying to deprive the 'poor' Muslims of the only 'wholesome food' within the latter's reach. All of them insisted with one voice that cow-slaughter was a 'established religious right' which they could not and should not forego. They went much farther. Cows meant for slaughter were taken out in processions through public thoroughfares in order to show contempt for Hindu sentiments. This led to some street riots in which some Hindus and some Muslims got killed.

The Muslim mass media raised a horrified howl of 'Islam in danger'. The 'majority', they said, was not only out to 'deprive' the 'minority' of its 'religious rights' of a long standing, but also bent upon a 'massacre' of the latter *en masse.* The howl was heard in other provinces in some of which Muslims had stopped cow-slaughter after the collapse of their political power. The Muslims in these provinces also rose in revolt against Hindu 'aggression'. They started reversing a settled trend. The British power was there to provide protection. The British courts had already given a decision that the government could not stop cow-slaughter by law. As a result, there were more riots in more places and more Hindus and Muslims got killed.

Hindus did not know how to meet this situation. They knew next to nothing about Islam. Otherwise, they would have pointed out that although Islam stood for a lot of slaughter — of animals as well as of human beings — the poor cow was nowhere in the picture. They would have quoted a hundred Islamic theologians who had recommended cow-slaughter not to secure heaven for the *mu'mins* but to humiliate the 'accursed' Hindus. Cow-slaughter was not an obligatory religions rite in Islam, conceding that Islam was a religion. On the contrary, it was an unequal privilege enjoyed by Muslims as a corollary of their military power or, conversely, a disability imposed on the *zimmīs* by an Islamic state. The case for cow-protection, therefore, went by default because Hindu society was not equipped to raise the issue to an ideological level.

NO MUSIC BEFORE THE MOSQUE

Meanwhile, another explosive controversy was moving to the fore. That was the matter of music before the mosque. A practice had prevailed earlier in areas which were ruled by Muslims that while Muslim processions could pass through purely Hindu localities, no Hindu procession was permitted to pass before a mosque, even if the mosque happened to be situated in a predominantly Hindu locality. Hindus were in no position to question this practice during the days of Muslim rule, and Muslims had taken it for granted. But now that Muslim rule was no more, some Hindus started having strong doubts about the sanctity of this practice. They started pointing out that Hindus were as good citizens as the Muslims and should have equal rights in the matter of public processions.

Once again, there was a horrified howl of 'Islam in danger'. It was pointed out by the Mullahs as well as Muslim scholars that Islam was a 'religion of peace' and that Muslims loved 'peace', particularly at the time of prayers, unlike the Hindu *dharam* in which there was too much ringing of bells and blowing of conches. Muslim musclemen threw an open challenge that no disturbance of the 'peace of Muslim prayers' would be permitted. Simultaneously, they started stocking the mosques with all sorts of missiles. A select band of Muslim butchers started sharpening their daggers and swords inside the same sanctuaries.

Hindus in some places persisted in taking out processions after informing the police. But as soon as a procession passed before a mosque, it was pelted with stones and other flying objects. Next, the butchers rushed out and stabbed some processionists. And before the police could intervene effectively, there was some bloodshed on both sides. The riot spread very soon to the rest of the town. Again, some Hindus and some Muslims got killed.

But once again, the Hindus lost the case by default. The Muslims needed to be told that the practice of not permitting processions to pass before a mosque had nothing to do with the 'peace of Muslim prayers'. Hindus could have quoted Caliph Umar and a hundred orthodox treatises like the *Hidāyah* to point out that prohibition of non-Muslim public celebrations, religious or otherwise, was one of the twenty-two disabilities which an Islamic state had always imposed on the hated *zimmīs*. Hindus under Muslim rule had not been permitted to celebrate their festivities loudly even inside their homes, not to speak of celebrating them on the streets. It was just another instance of an unjust privilege usurped by Muslims in the period of their political supremacy.

The Islamic state was no more. The British rule was supposed to be based upon equality of all citizens before the law. Yet, the Muslims got away with an unjust privilege acquired by them earlier. Those in charge of law and order could not see the justice in the Hindu point of view. They also enacted a law which prohibited music before a mosque. The law has been retained on the statute book of an independent India where Hindus are supposed to be in an overwhelming majority

UPROAR OVER URDU

The national demand for cow-protection and passing of processions before the mosques had challenged some unjust privileges which the residues of Islamic imperialism had continued to retain in the name of their 'religion'. These demands, however, were not likely to damage their economic or social status in any manner. They could laugh in private at their strategy of trouncing the Hindus and seeking mass Muslim support, while pulling long faces in public. But the next thing that happened looked like hitting them where it could really hurt. That was the so-called Hindi Resolution passed by the Government of U.P. in April, 1900. The residues of Islamic imperialism now raised a howl as if heavens had fallen.

So long as Muslim rule had prevailed in many parts of the country, Persian had been the language of government and administration. All public services had been the monopoly of Muslims, mostly of foreign descent, except at the lowest levels where some Hindus were also allowed to serve after learning Persian. The ranks of the foreign Muslim fraternity had continued to be reinforced by fresh arrivals from all over the Islamic world. The vast majority of natives, Hindus as well as Muslim converts, had been helplessly dependent on scribes who knew Persian, whenever and wherever they came in contact with the administrative machinery.

The situation changed with the change of masters. The British replaced Persian by English in the higher echelons and by Urdu at the lower levels. The residues of Islamic imperialism had resented this change also but got reconciled to it because their privileged position in public services had not been affected. They began feeling uncomfortable only when Urdu also started getting replaced by local languages like Bengali, Marathi, Tamil and Telugu, etc. Muslims were not in a majority in these provinces except in Bengal, where also there was hardly any Muslim middle class and the Muslim peasantry had never known any language other than its native Bengali.

Meanwhile, pressure of public opinion was building up in Bihar, the Central Provinces and U.P., where Hindi, the mother tongue of the common people, had all along received a step-motherly treatment. Urdu was replaced by Hindi in the Central Provinces in 1872, and in Bihar in 1881. But the Government of U.P. continued to cold-shoulder Hindi due to the influence of Sir Syed Ahmad Khan and his Aligarh lobby. It was only after 1894, when Antony MacDonell became the Lieutenant Governor, that a long-standing and just demand of the local people came up for an active review. But even a sympathetic Governor could not go the whole hog in favour of Hindi. He converted the language controversy into a competition of rival scripts. Nagari script was now placed on par with the Persian script, and both were made compulsory for all those who aspired for government service at certain levels where English was not essential.

It was only a small concession. The Muslims were still free to write Urdu in Persian script. But even this small concession to the common people was too much for the residues of Islamic imperialism. They raised a strong protest that their 'lofty language' was being 'brought down' to the level of '*Hindī gandī*'. They pointed out that Hindus had been learning Urdu all these years, and that it was only their 'hatred' for Islam and the Muslims which was leading them to neglect it in future. They added that next to Arabic and Persian, Urdu was the language of their 'religion and culture', and that Urdu could be written only in the Persian script. And they concluded that while the 'prosperous and wily' Hindus had many avenues of employment, the 'poor and simple' Muslims were solely dependent on government patronage.

MacDonell was not impressed. He told the Muslims that they already had their communal quota in terms of which a mere fourteen per cent of the provincial population had monopolised thirty-seven-and-a-half per cent of government jobs. But the Muslims were far from being mollified. They became extremely agitated under the leadership provided again by the Aligarh lobby. A pathetic couplet, composed by Mohsin-ul-Mulk, Secretary of the Aligarh College, now started circulating among the Muslims all over the province:

chal sāth ke hasrat dil-i-mahrūm se nikle,
āshiq kā janāzā hai zarā dhūm se nikle.

(Walk with [the bier] so that the longing [for love] may not linger in the hollowed heart. This is the funeral procession of your lover. Let it proceed with some song and dance.)

URDU HAD REMAINED A FOREIGN LANGUAGE

Before we pass on to the storm raised over Urdu by the residues of Islamic imperialism, we should like to quote what Professor Aziz Ahmad has said about this language. He writes: "The poets of Delhi, proud of the 'pure' Urdu of the imperial camp, rejected the Dakani principle and practice of borrowing extensively from the Indian languages, especially if these borrowings were related to Hindu religion, culture and world-view... In this process imagery was drawn exclusively from Persian precedents, *i.e.*, from the unseen and unexperienced sights, sounds and smells of Persia and Central Asia, rejecting totally the Indian sights, sounds and sensuous experience as materials regarded not sublime enough for poetic expression... It was a desperate unconscious clinging to the origins of the symbols of Muslim India's cultural experience which had begun abroad, and an instinctive fear of being submerged into the Hindu cultural milieu. These modes of aesthetic appreciation, rooted so deeply in the essence of universal Islamic culture, remained more or less incomprehensible to the Hindu mind. Its reaction has been summed up by [S.K.] Chatterjee: 'Throughout the whole range of Urdu literature in its first phase ... the atmosphere of this literature is provokingly un-Indian — it is that of Persia. Early Urdu poets never so much as mention the great physical features of India — its Himalayas, its rivers like the Ganges, the Jamuna, the Sindhu, the Godavari, etc; but of course mountains and streams of Persia, and rivers of Central Asia are always there. Indian flowers, Indian plants are unknown; only Persian flowers and plants which the poet could see only in a garden. There was a deliberate shutting of the eye to everything Indian, to everything not mentioned or treated in Persian poetry... A language and literature which came to base itself upon an ideology which denied on the Indian soil the very existence of India and Indian culture, could not but be met with a challenge from some of the Indian adherents of their national culture; and that challenge was in the form of highly Sanskritized Hindi'."[2]

YET URDU WON A VICTORY

This was the language which the residues of Islamic imperialism wanted to impose upon the common people, Hindus and Muslim converts, till the end of time. Some years earlier, they had organised a Mohammedan Anglo-Oriental Defence Association of Upper India. Mohsin-ul-Mulk converted this body into an Urdu Defence Association. It was decided to call a conference of leading Muslims from all over North India to discuss the Hindi Resolution and to draft a representation to the Lieutenant Governor. Meanwhile, leading Muslims had spread out in the district towns of U.P. to whip up a mass hysteria. The cries of 'Islam in danger' were heard as far as Lahore in the Punjab, Dacca in Bengal, Bombay in Maharashtra, and Madras in South India. Finally, a conference was held at Lucknow in August, 1900. It was attended by 400 delegates from the Punjab, Bombay Presidency, Central Provinces, U.P. and elsewhere. The Mullahs, landlords, merchants, lawyers, journalists and others who had flocked to the conference called upon the 'Muslim masses' to defend their 'religion and culture' with all their might. Mohsin-ul-Mulk thundered: "Although we have not the might of the pen our hands are still strong enough to wield the might of the sword."

Nothing came out of the Hindi Resolution of the government. MacDonell was soon succeeded by LaTouche who wrote to the Viceroy, Lord Curzon, that MacDonell "went too far in acknowledging Hindi as a language" For a long time afterwards, no bilingual examinations were held and no government orders were issued in the Nagari script. In fact, the number of Muslims in government services increased in subsequent years.

The cat came out of the bag in October 1906 when the residues of Islamic imperialism, who had held another conference in Lucknow in the meanwhile, drew up a Memorandum to the Viceroy, Lord Minto. The Memorandum was presented by a delegation of 35 Muslim no-

---

[2] Aziz Ahmad, *Studies In Islamic Culture*, Oxford, 1964, pp. 252-55.

tables led by the Agha Khan. It was a prelude to the formation of the Muslim League, later on in the same year. The Memorandum reminded the British rulers that the Muslims had been the ruling class for a long time and requested that the government "give due consideration to the position that they [Muslims] occupied in India a little more than a hundred years ago". It insisted that the 'political importance' of the Muslim community be conceded. Political importance, in turn, was spelled out in the following words: "The political importance of a community to a considerable extent gains strength or suffers detriment according to the position that the members of that community occupy in the service of the State."

Professor Francis Robinson sums up the situation when he says that "Aligarh College and the All India Muslim League were founded to preserve a strong position, not to improve a weak one" and that "It was the threat of becoming backward, rather than backwardness itself, which encouraged U.P. Muslims to organize for politics, and their power in the province helped them to do so with effect."[3] Backwardness in this context meant becoming equal to the rest of their countrymen — a prospect which the residues of Islamic imperialism have always dreaded as worse than death.

---

[3] Francis Robinson, *Separatism Among Indian Muslims*, Delhi, 1975, p. 346.

Chapter X
THE SEPARATIST SEWER POLLUTES THE NATIONAL MAINSTREAM

There is one chapter in the history of our freedom movement against British imperialism which has caused considerable confusion. This chapter opened with the signing of the Lucknow Pact in December 1916, and closed with the withdrawal of the first Non-Cooperation Movement by Mahatma Gandhi in February 1922. Many politicians and historians have looked back wistfully to those 'wonderful days of Hindu-Muslim unity' when the Indian National Congress and the All-India Muslim League held their annual sessions in the same city and at the same time, passed similar anti-imperialist resolutions, and raised similar slogans. Few political scientists have cared to interpret correctly and consistently the detailed documentation which has been available for quite some time regarding the motives of the Muslim League and, later on, of the Mullahs in making a common cause with the Congress. It looks like a wilful refusal to face facts which sound unsavoury.

Shri H.V. Seshadri also seems to share this confusion when he refers to 'A New Breeze Among Muslims'.[1] He disapproves of the Lucknow Pact which he very aptly describes as a 'Sanction to Separatism'.[2] He also rejects the Khilafat agitation as 'A Himalayan Error', which is a very sound summing up of a suicidal step which was taken by the national movement under the leadership of Mahatma Gandhi.[3] Yet he seems to welcome the 'New Breeze' which brought the Muslim League and the Mullas close to the Congress and led to an ignominious surrender of cherished principles on the part of the latter. It is obvious that there is some contradiction somewhere.

THERE WAS NO NEW BREEZE AMONG MUSLIMS

Shri Seshadri would not have landed himself in this contradiction if he had gone a little farther afield, and probed a little deeper into the Muslim mind as it was working after the passing of the so-called Hindi Resolution by the U.P. Government in April 1900. In that case, he could not have avoided the conclusion that there was no 'New Breeze', and that what was still blowing among the Muslims was the old and stale wind of separatism. The residues of Islamic imperialism had not moved a jot from placing Islamic causes above the freedom and welfare

---

[1] *The Tragic Story of Partition,* p.47
[2] Ibid., p.54
[3] Ibid., Chapter 8.

of the Indian people as a whole. Their goals were still the same as in the earlier phase when Sir Syed Ahmed Khan had presided over their perfidy. It was only their strategy for securing those goals which had undergone a shift.

It is true that the residues of Islamic imperialism were now writhing with bitterness against the British. But this bitterness was not caused because the British had enslaved India and were exploiting the Indian people. On the contrary, this bitterness was born because of being brought down to earth at a time when they had got used to riding a high horse. They were feeling outraged that their British patrons should have thought it fit to 'betray' them in spite of so many services rendered by them for so many years. The psychology of the residues of Islamic imperialism at that time will become clear as soon as we examine the causes in the context of which they had developed the sense of complaint against the British.

CAUSES OF MUSLIM BITTERNESS AGAINST THE BRITISH

The primary cause which excited bitterness against the British among a certain section of Muslims in India was Pan-Islamic. This bitterness had been growing since the Russio-Turkish War of 1876-78 when this section expected Britain to side with Turkey. But Britain had 'failed' them, and they had invited "the Sultan of Turkey to forge an alliance with the Mahdi of Sudan and invade India".[4] There was an interval of rejoicing when Turkey defeated Greece in 1897. "The custom of mentioning the name of the Sultan of Turkey with titles in the *Khutbah* started at this time... He was the Caliph and as such the Commander of all the Faithful wherever they lived."[5] But the rejoicing proved short-lived. The Muslim countries were increasingly getting into trouble everywhere, and the Caliph, far from being in a position to help them, was himself sinking into deep waters. The British had occupied Egypt; the French and the British had reached an agreement with regard to Morocco; the Russians and the British had signed a Convention with regard to Persia; the Italians had invaded Tripoli (present-day Libya) without any opposition from the British; Greece, Bulgaria, Serbia and Montenegro had fought a war against Turkey and defeated their old imperialist enemy while Britain kept looking at it all as a sympathetic spectator. The residues of Islamic imperialism started shrieking that the Government of Great Britain had become 'an enemy

---

[4] Ishtiaq Husain Qureshi, *Ulema in Politics*, Delhi reprint, 1985, p. 242.

[5] Ibid.

of Islam', and that it was the duty of all Muslims in India not only to hate but also to destroy that government.

They were not angry with the Government of Great Britain because that Government had enslaved their own motherland; they were angry because that Government was playing a neutral or partisan role regarding the fate of some far off Muslim countries. They had not only no objection to Turkey being an imperialist power which had forcibly occupied many foreign lands in Africa, Asia and Europe including those of the Arabs; they also admired Turkey for being the bastion of Islamic power and the seat of the Caliph (*amir-ul-mu'minīn*). And they were denouncing Great Britain for not aiding and abetting Turkey to retain its hold over its prison-house of nationalities. On the other hand, they had no sympathy to spare for many other nations all over the world that were groaning under the yoke of Belgian, Dutch, French and British imperialism. The only fault of these other nations was that they were not Muslim.

Next, the Muslim in India had found a few causes for complaint against the British Government in India. The first cause was the annulment of the Partition of Bengal in 1911. The residues of Islamic imperialism were stunned into silence when this British decision was announced at the imperial *durbār* in Delhi. The next moment, they started shrieking that the British had betrayed their best and most faithful allies, and that the Muslims had been thrown into the gutter after being led up the garden path. There was not a single statement from any Muslim leader that a great wrong had been undone, and that the rights of which their fellow countrymen had been wrongfully deprived had been restored.

The second cause was a refusal by the British Government to concede that the Anglo-Oriental Mohammedan College at Aligarh should be converted into a university which could affiliate Muslim educational institutions from all over India. The Government was prepared to help them build either a residential campus or a regional university which would affiliate all colleges, Muslim or otherwise, spread over a certain area. This was fully in keeping with the prevailing law and practice governing the constitution of all universities in what was then known as British India. But the residues of all Islamic imperialism had become incurably addicted to enjoying unequal privileges. They had been pressing the Government to grant them a special charter for their proposed leviathan. This the Government refused to do for fear of raising a hornet's nest among other communities. And the residues of Islamic imperialism started shrieking again that they had been betrayed.

MUSLIMS STAGE AN ANTI-CLIMAX

There were some other developments, major and minor, such as that of the mosque at Kanpur. We need not go into all of them here. What matters is that, taken together, they provide a key to an understanding of the anti-climax staged by the residues of Islamic imperialism not long after they had circulated the *Lal Ishtahār* (Red Pamphlet) all over Bengal in the wake of the first Muslim League meeting at Dacca in December 1906. The *Ishtahār* was a handiwork of Samiullah, the Nawab of Dacca, and his henchmen who had hosted the delegates to the meeting of delegates from all over India. It was obvious that the anti-Congress crusade launched by Sir Syed Ahmed in the closing years of the 19th century was being converted quite fast into an all-out anti-Hindu *jihād*. The *Ishtahār* had proclaimed in wringing tones: "Ye Musalmans, arise, awake! Do not read in the same schools with the Hindus. Do not touch any article manufactured by the Hindus. Do not give any employment to the Hindus. Do not accept any degrading office under a Hindu. You are ignorant, but if you acquire knowledge you can send all Hindus to *Jahannum* (Hell). You form the majority of the population in this province. The Hindu has no wealth of his own and has made himself rich only by despoiling you of your wealth. If you become sufficiently enlightened, the Hindus will starve and soon become Mohammedans."[6]

Early in 1907, Muslim hooligans had let loose a reign of terror against defenceless Hindus in the countryside of East Bengal. H.W. Nevison who visited India as a representative of *The Manchester Guardian* had reported: "Priestly Mullahs went through the country preaching the revival of Islam and proclaiming to the villagers that the British Government was on the Mohammedan side, that the Law Courts had been specially suspended for three months and no penalty would be exacted for violence done to the Hindus, or for the loot of Hindu shops or the abduction of Hindu widows. A Red Pamphlet was everywhere circulated maintaining the same wild doctrine... In Comilla, Jamalpur and a few other places, rather serious riots occurred. A few lives were lost, temples desecrated, images broken, shops plundered, and many widows carried off. Some of the towns were deserted, the Hindu population took refuge in any *pukka* houses, women spent nights hidden in tanks, the crime known as 'group-rape' increased and throughout the country districts, there reigned a general terror, which still prevailed

[6] Cited in R.C. Majumdar (ed.), *History and Culture of the Indian People*, Volume XI, Bombay, 1978, p.54.

at the time of my visit."[7]

This was the atmosphere in most of the Muslim majority areas when the anti-climax came all of a sudden. The anti-climax was staged by the residues of Islamic imperialism not because they had renounced their separatist game; it was staged in order to play that game in a new manner amidst a new configuration of forces. The British Government in India was no longer in a position to pamper them any further because of the rising tide of national resistance. The British government in Great Britain was not in a position to support Pan-Islamic causes because of its own international interests and alignments. But the residues of Islamic imperialism were incapable of understanding the difficulties of their patron. They could not get over the obsession that the causes espoused by them were the only causes worth espousing by everybody else.

Even so, Muslims in India were hesitating in making a decision, and were debating among themselves whether they should join hands with the Hindu *kāfirs*. What decided the issue for them was the advice they received from their mentors abroad. "Both the Afghans and the Turks," records Ishtiaq Husain Qureshi, "had impressed upon their leaders the stark necessity of gaining the cooperation of the Hindus... It had been impressed upon them that the citadel of British power in Asia was India, which made all the Muslim countries in Asia vulnerable to attack and encroachment... Therefore, whatever the cost involved, the British power must be dislodged from that citadel. They, like the Hindus, wanted freedom, but if the Hindus were to play false after the departure of the British, at least the Muslim countries will be able to breathe freely. The Muslims of the Subcontinent wanted to be partners in the freedom of their habitat as well as in the liberty of the rest of the Muslim world, but if the glory of Islam and prosperity of other Muslim lands could be built only upon their own misery and deprivation, they thought the price was not high to pay..."[8]

That is how there was something dramatic about the anti-climax when it came. The very same people who had so far frowned upon even the idea of an agitation against the British Government, were now advocating that anti-government agitation was the only way. The most fanatic anti-Congress elements had suddenly launched a campaign for a common front between the Indian National Congress and the Muslim League against what they described as British imperialism for the first time. The most persistent preachers of hatred against Hindus were now

---

[7] H.W. Nevison, *The New Spirit in India*, London, 1908, p. 192 and 193.
[8] Ishtiq Husain Qureshi, *Ulema in Politics*, pp. 259-60.

pleading for Hindu-Muslim unity. This was an altogether new language in the mouths of Muslim leaders.

NATIONAL LEADERSHIP WALKS INTO THE TRAP

This new language in the Muslim press and from the Muslim political platforms was hailed heartily by the Indian National Congress. Nobody in the Congress noticed the motives which were moving the residues of Islamic imperialism towards the national mainstream. Nobody among the Congress stalwarts studied the psychology at the back of new slogans which the residues of Islamic imperialism were now raising from the housetops. Nobody in the Nationalist ranks bothered to find out whether the 'race of conquerors' had shed any of its hauteur, and whether their new anti-imperialist stance had any positive content. On the contrary, the Indian National Congress rushed headlong, first into the Lucknow Pact and then into the Khilafat agitation.

The Lucknow Pact signed by Lokmanya Tilak on behalf of the Congress and by M.A. Jinnah on behalf of the Muslim League, put a seal of approval on all the illegitimate gains made by the residues of Islamic imperialism during an earlier period when they were basking in the sunshine of British patronage. The most notable of these gains was separate electorates which had been conferred upon them by the Minto-Morley Reforms in 1909. The Congress had been resisting separate electorates so far. Now, all of a sudden, it conceded them not only in practice but also in principle. And what was worse, the Congress also conceded weightages to the Muslims in all those provinces where they were in a minority. This was a very vicious principle which even the British Government had refused to recognise in spite of being pressurised for long by the residues of Islamic imperialism.

The Khilafat agitation in which the Congress agreed to participate compromised very seriously the principle according to which the achievement of self-government for India was the primary aim of the national movement. The Congress, particularly Mahatma Gandhi, was now prepared to give primacy to the preservation of the Caliphate at Constantinople, and thus placed the national movement at the disposal of Pan-Islamism. The continuation or otherwise of the Caliphate was not even remotely related to any national interest or objective.

A NEW STAGE IN THE NATIONAL MOVEMENT

And these surrenders were made by the Congress at a time when the national movement had attained a new stage, and had forced the British Government to annul the Partition of Bengal. The Congress was no longer a congregation of some outstanding personalities passing some pious resolutions at annual conferences and then retiring to their private pursuits. It had become a mass movement, particularly in Bengal, Maharashtra and the Punjab, and had acquired a potential for developing along the same lines in other provinces. This becomes clear as soon as we cast a glance at the Swadeshi Movement.

The Swadeshi Movement which had sprung up spontaneously in response to the Partition of Bengal in 1905, was not only a new stage in the fight for freedom from British imperialism but also a radical departure from the beaten track along which the freedom movement had travelled so far. The freedom movement now had not only attained a new high but also acquired a truly national temper. The new direction towards which the nation was now headed was symbolized by the battle-cry of *Vande Mātaram*.

This was not a negative slogan like boycott and non-cooperation. Nor was it a purely political platform like passive resistance. It was much more. It was a mighty *mantra* pulsating with positive aspirations of an ancient people whose primary pursuit had been the perfection of human life in accordance with a vast spiritual vision. Swadeshi and National Education were only the first manifestations of this *mantra*. Many more manifestations were maturing in the national mind, which had now awakened to its own native powers and potentialities.

What was more significant, the Swadeshi Movement had soon spread from Bengal to several other parts of India. It had thrown up a new type of leaders such as Bipin Chandra Pal in Bengal, Lokmanya Tilak in Maharashtra, and Lala Lajpat Rai in the Punjab, to name only the most notable. It had inspired revolutionary activities in India as well as abroad. It had drawn its inspiration from a mighty scripture like the Gita. Its foremost exponent was Sri Aurobindo whose clarion call in the columns of the *Bande Mataram* and the *Karmayogin* had raised politics to the level of spiritual *sādhanā*.

The Swadeshi Movement had also found a mighty minstrel in Rabindranath who sang his epic songs in homage to Shivaji and Banda Bairagi at this time. In his soul-stirring poetry, the battles fought against Islamic imperialism by the Rajputs, the Marathas, the Jats, the Sikhs, and several other communities in the national complex, had become a backdrop for battles being fought against British imperialism. The hoary history of Hindu society and culture had now started acquiring a new meaning — it had become the history of an immortal nation which had made great contributions in all fields of human creativity; which had fashioned some splendid social, political, economic and cultural institutions from out of its innermost soul; which had fought and frustrated several foreign invaders; and which was now rising again to hold its head high in the comity of nations and to play its characteristic role in world affairs. Such a nation could surely look at it past with a lot of legitimate pride. Such a nation could surely look towards its future with some measure of self-confidence.

Shri Seshadri provides an explanation of the surrenders made by the Congress, starting in 1916. He has laid his probing finger squarely on that soft spot in the Congress psychology which had made the Congress prone to suffering such a paralytic stroke. He writes: "The Congress, befitting its name of Indian National Congress, had declared itself a representative body of all groups, religious or otherwise, in the country. It was, therefore, its pre-eminent duty to stand steadfast by its commitment to the interests and integrity of the nation as a whole and never succumb to the pressure tactics of any particular section of whatever denomination. However, to the nation's misfortune, the Congress was trapped in the coils of the theories of 'composite nation' and 'composite culture' and infected with an inferiority complex that unless all communities came to its platform it could not become a national organization. It became nervous at the prospect of being dubbed 'communal' if Hindus alone participated in its activities."[9]

He quotes Surendernath Banerjee to reveal the ridiculous extent to which the Congress could go in order to attract some Muslims to its platform. Banerjee had written in 1926: "Our critics regarded the National Congress as a Hindu Congress, and the opposition papers described it as such. We were straining every nerve to secure the co-operation of our Mohammedan fellow countrymen... We sometime paid the fares of Muhammedan delegates and offered them some other facilities."[10]

Shri Seshadri also cites the eyewitness account of Swami Shraddhananda regarding 'some other facilities' which were provided at the Congress session in 1899 at Lucknow. Swamiji also wrote as follows in 1926: "Tickets were issued to every Muslim *Waiz* delegate free of charge. Messing charges of Rs.10 per head, too, were not charged to the Muslim delegates while they were served with all the delicacies of *Dastarkhan*. And these *Waiz* delegates stopped in the pandal only a few minutes in the beginning and were to be found enjoying creature comforts under the refreshment *shamianah* outside the pandal for the rest of the sitting... The majority of Muslim delegates

---

[9] *The Tragic Story of Partition*, p. 51.
[10] Ibid.

had donned gold, silver or silk-embroidered *chogas* (flowing robes) over their ordinary coarse suits of wearing apparel. It was rumoured that these *chogas* had been lent by Hindu moneyed men for Congress *tamasha*."[11]

That was how the sewer of Muslim separatism was permitted, almost invited, to pollute the national mainstream. Surdas, the saint-poet of the 16th century, had envisaged the purification of a sewer (*nāro*) as soon as it poured itself into a stream (*nadī*). But what happened in the case of the Congress was a contamination of the stream by the sewer. The sewer gave some of its own colour and chemistry to the stream. The national mainstream not only lost its own purity; it also became putrid by its contact with Muslim separatism. Ever since, the national mainstream has continued to breed whole colonies of anti-national parasites. The infection has by now become a creeping cancer, so much so that the very mention of native nationalism now stinks as 'Hindu communalism' in the nostrils of the Indian National Congress.

---

[11] Ibid.

CHAPTER 11
THE BEHAVIOUR PATTERN PATENTED BY ISLAM

On August 4, 1920, Mahatma Gandhi had written as follows in his *Young India*: "My advice to my Hindu brethren is: Simply help the Mussalmans in their sorrow in a generous and self-sacrificing spirit without counting the cost and you will automatically save the cow... *Islam is a noble faith*. Trust it and its followers. We must hold it a crime for any Hindu to talk to them about cow-protection or any other help in our religious matters, while the *Khilafat* struggle is going on."[1]

But one day during his 21 days fast in September 1924, he confessed his error to Mahadev Desai in the following words: "My error? Why, I may be charged with having committed a breach of faith with the Hindus. I asked them to lay their lives and their property at the disposal of the Mussalmans for the protection of their Holy Places. Even to-day I am asking them to practise *Ahimsa*, to settle quarrels by dying but not by killing. And what do I find to be the result? How many temples have been desecrated? How many sisters came to me with complaints? As I was saying to Hakimji [Ajmal Khan] yesterday, Hindu women are in mortal fear of Mussalman *goondas*. I had a letter from... *How can I bear the way in which his little children were molested*? How can I now ask Hindus to put up with everything patiently? I gave the assurance that the friendship with Mussalmans was bound to bear fruit. I asked them to befriend them, regardless of results. It is not in my power to make good that assurance. And yet I must ask the Hindus even to-day to die rather than kill. I can only do so by laying down my own life. I can teach them the way to die by my own example."[2]

This was the behaviour pattern of a gentleman who had put his trust in the pledges given by the foremost Muslim leaders in India while they were seeking his support for a Pan-Islamic cause. The gentleman had discovered that he had been duped. But still he was in no mood to call for a repudiation of his reading of Islam, or for revenge. Many people at that time had found fault with this behaviour pattern, as many other people continue to do today. But no one has ever questioned the sincerity of the Mahatma's motives. And it has been conceded by everyone that he was not out to deceive the Muslims, that he had no ulterior designs, and that he never harboured any intention of using the other party as a pawn for his own purposes.

---

[1] Emphasis added.
[2] Mahadev Desai, *Day to Day with Gandhi*, Volume 4, p. 165. Emphasis added.

On the other hand, we have the behaviour pattern exhibited by Abdul Bari, the leading Mullah from Firangi Mahal in Lucknow, and the topmost spokesmen for the Muslims during the Khilafat agitation. In September 1920, he had advised the Muslims as follows: "The Muslim honour would be at stake if they forget the co-operation of the Hindus. I for my part will say that we should stop killing cows, irrespective of their cooperation, because we are children of the same soil. As a maulvi I say that in voluntarily stopping cow-killing we shall not offend against the canons of our religion. Nothing has so helped the Hindu-Muslim unity as the Hindus' co-operation with us on the Khilafat question."[3]

The same Abdul Bari spoke in a different tone in September 1923. Professor Francis Robinson reports: "Abdul Bari, the erstwhile apostle of Hindu-Muslim unity, came to the fore again. *Now he spoke the language of the zealot.* He urged the Muslims to sacrifice cows without regard to Hindu feelings, and declared: 'If the commandments of the Shariat are to be trampled under foot then it will be the same to us whether the decision is arrived on the plains of Delhi or on the hilltops of Simla. We are determined to non-cooperate with every enemy of Islam, be he in Anatolia or Arabia or at Agra or Benares."[4]

The immediate provocation for Abdul Bari's outburst was the Shuddhi Movement started by Swami Shraddhananda in the summer of 1923. Swamiji in turn had been led to pursue this path in response to a book, *Fātimī Dāwat-i-Islām*, by Hasan Nizami, another Muslim Mullah hailing from the *dargah* of Nizam-ud-Din Awliya, the famous Sufi of Delhi. Swamiji had written a pamphlet, *The Hour of Danger*, in which he had warned Hindu society to be on its guard against mischievous Muslim machinations. According to his biographer, J.T.F. Jordens, "In his pamphlet the Swami went on to show how Nizami in his own introduction referred to his consultations with many Muslim leaders, including the Agha Khan, and how all had agreed that the publication of his work should remain a carefully kept secret, within the Muslim community. The single purpose of the pamphlet was to describe all the means, fair and foul, by which Hindus could be induced to become Muslims. It said that the attack should strongly concentrate on the untouchables because 'if all untouchable castes become Muslims then the Muslim part (of the population) will become equal to that of the Hindus'. The Swami felt that he had uncovered a giant conspiracy. His pamphlet consisted practically entirely of quotations from Nizami's work, show-

---

[3] Cited by H.V. Seshadri from Ram Gopal, *Indian Muslims*, p. 138.

[4] Francis Robinson, op.cit. p. 339.

ing how all Muslims should be involved in the fight for the spread of Islam: how *pirs*, fakirs, politicians, peasants, zamindars, hakims, etc. could be used and what their allotted task should be. It also stressed the need for secrecy and for an extensive spy network.'[5]

Abdul Bari clean forgot that Swami Shraddhananda had unconditionally supported the Khilafat agitation under the leadership of Mahatma Gandhi. It was Swamiji who had bared his breast in Chandni Chowk on March 30, 1919, and dared the British soldiers to try their bullets on him. It was Swamiji whom the Muslims of Delhi had invited to address them from the *mimbar* of the Jama Masjid on March 31, 1919. Abdul Bari should have denounced Hasan Nizami who had hatched a plot against the Hindus without any provocation whatsoever on the part of the latter. But the self-righteous Mullah and the authoritative interpreter of the Shariat, had done just the opposite. He had joined his voice with that of the other Mullahs in egging upon a Muslim fanatic to murder Swami Shraddhananda. The Mullahs of Deoband had offered special prayers for the soul of the assassin.

In fact, the Mullahs had been fretting and fuming ever since Mahatma Gandhi had withdrawn in February 1922 the Non-Cooperation Movement which he had led in support of the Khilafat agitation. They were in search of an excuse for reversing their *fatwa* against cow-killing and for co-operation with the Hindus. That *fatwa* had gone against the whole history of Islam in India in spite of the brave face which the Khilafat leaders had put on it.[6] The Shuddhi Movement had provided that excuse and the Mullahs had plumped for it. They were swift to terminate what Ishtiq Husain Qureshi has called "A Brief Honeymoon".[7] Now they incited Muslim mobs to stage riots all over the country. Hindus were to be taught how to behave towards the 'master race'.

This was the behaviour pattern of hoodlums who got extremely annoyed with the donkey which had carried them so far but which did not have the strength left to carry the load any farther. This was the behaviour pattern of gangsters who felt frustrated because the victims of their deep-laid designs had seen through their wiles and refused to be duped any longer. But, at the same time, these Mullahs were in the forefront of Muslim society. Leading politicians like the Ali Brothers

[5] J.T.F. Jordens, *Swami Shradhananda: His Life and Causes*, New Delhi, 1981, Pp.140.41.

[6] The Mullahs in India have always regarded cow-slaughter as one of the noblest (*azīm*) practices of Islam. As late as 3 April 1986, Ali Mian of Lucknow, the top-most Mullah, has harangued the Muslims in India not to give up this practice (Arun Shourie, *A Secular Agenda*, New Delhi, 1993, p. 346).

[7] Ishtiaq Husain Qureshi, *Ulema in Politics*, Chapter X.

had bowed before them in reverence. The behaviour pattern of the exponents and custodians of Islam, therefore, cannot but lead us to the inescapable conclusion that Islam itself has always been, and remains, a thinly veiled theorisation of gangsterism.

RABINDRANATH ON HINDU-MUSLIM UNITY

One aspect of this behaviour pattern had been noticed by the great poet, Rabindranath, who was reported as follows in an interview to *The Times of India* published on April 18, 1924: "Another very important fact which according to the poet was making it almost impossible for Hindu-Mohammedan unity to become an accomplished fact was that the Mohammedans could not confine their patriotism to any one country. The poet said that he had very frankly asked many Mohammedans whether, in the event of any Mohammedan power invading India, they would stand side by side with their Hindu neighbours to defend their common land. He could not be satisfied with the reply he got from them. He said that he could definitely state that even men like Mr. Mohammed Ali had declared that under no circumstances was it permissible for any Mohammedan, whatever his country might be, to stand against any other Mohammedan."[8]

LALA LAJPAT RAI ON THE SAME THEME

At about the same time Lala Lajpat Rai came to the conclusion that this behaviour pattern had its primary source in the Quran and the Hadis. Lalaji wrote as follows in a confidential letter to Deshbandhu C.R. Das: "I have devoted most of my time during the last six months to the study of Muslim history and Muslim Law and I am inclined to think that Hindu-Muslim unity is neither possible nor practicable... Assuming and admitting the sincerity of the Mohammedan leaders in the Non-Co-operation Movement, I think their religion provides an effective bar to anything of the kind. There is no finer Mohammedan than Hakim [Ajmal Khan] Sahab, but can any Muslim leader override the Koran? I can only hope that my reading of the Islamic Law is incorrect and nothing would relieve me more than to be convinced that it is so... I do honestly and sincerely believe in the necessity and desirability of Hindu-Muslim unity. I am also fully prepared to trust the Muslim leaders, but what about the injunctions of the Koran and the Hadis? The leaders cannot override them."[9]

---

[8] Quoted by A. Ghosh in, 'Making of the Muslim Psyche' in Devendra Swamp (ed.), *Politics of Conversion*, New Delhi, 1986, p. 148.

[9] Ibid., p. 147.

SARAT CHANDRA SUMS UP THE SUBJECT

Shri Sarat Chandra Chatterji, the noted Bengali novelist and a Congressman of long standing, had commented on the overt behaviour of Muslims ever since Islam arrived in India. Pained by the humiliations which Muslim hooligans had heaped on Hindus in the countryside of East Bengal, he had written as follows in October, 1926: "If we go by the lessons of history we have to accept that the goal of Hindu-Muslim unity is a mirage. When Muslims first entered India, they looted the country, destroyed the temples, broke the idols, raped the women and heaped innumberable indignities on the people of this country. Today it appears that such noxious behaviour has entered the bone-marrow of Muslims. Unity can be achieved among equals. In view of the big gap between the cultural level of Hindus and Muslims which can hardly be bridged, I am of the view that Hindu-Muslim unity which could not be achieved during the last thousand years will not materialise during the ensuing thousand years. If we are to drive away the English people depending upon this elusive capital of Hindu-Muslim unity, I would rather advise its postponement."[10]

HINDU FAILURE TO UNDERSTAND ISLAM

In an article in *Young India* dated May 29, 1924, Mahatma Gandhi had himself noted that "*my own experience confirms that the Mussalman as a rule is a bully*". Only he did not trace this Muslim behaviour pattern to the tenets of Islam which continued to be a "noble faith" for him till he himself was consumed by the flames ignited by this faith. But the Mahatma was neither the first nor the last Hindu to commit this mistake about Islam. Hindu society has been a wilful victim of this folly ever since Islam arrived India on the shoulders of Arab armies in the second half of the 7th century AD.

This imperialist ideology of terrorism has been in India for the last thirteen centuries and more. But with the exception of Swami Dayananda and the Arya Samaj, no Hindu thinker or organization has made a serious or systematic study of its mind or methods. The Hindu response to Islam has invariably been a series of slogans — Ram and Rahim are one and the same, Allah and Ishwar describe the same Supreme Power, Kashi and Ka'abah are equally holy, the mosque is a variation of the *mandir* even when the former has been built on the site and with the debris of the latter, *namāz* is another name for *upāsanā* (worship), in short, Islam is as good as *Sanātana Dharma*.

---

[10] Ibid., p. 148.

What is worse, Hindu society has fallen into an inveterate habit of white-washing and wishing away the dark deeds of Islam by dressing them up in Hindu verbiage. Hindus never allow the spokesmen of Islam to speak for themselves. Instead, they interpret Islam in terms of the Indian spiritual traditions, and try their utmost to force this diabolical creed into divine moulds. And they flaunt this habit as a *sine qua non* of their liberalism and large-heartedness, their capacity to digest and transform into nector even the most potent poison.

Hindu society has never paused to find out how Islamic theologians respond to its cherished slogans and sentiments. It has always been in a hurry to sell some patent prescriptions like *sarva-dharma-samabhāva* so that the slogans may be put into practice unilaterally. That is why all Hindu slogans have so far fallen on deaf ears, or have invited contempt from the Muslims who know their *Dīn* A to Z. That is why all Hindu prescriptions have proved to be costly mistakes. That is why a great Hindu like Mahatma Gandhi who succeeded against all other odds, ended as a total and tragic failure when it came to the followers of Islam.

We blamed the British for Hindu-Muslim conflict so long as the British controlled this country. Then we lulled ourselves into the fond belief that the 'communal problem' had been finally solved by the Partition in 1947, and that we could settle down to solving the problems of poverty and social injustice. But the belief has been shattered by the increasing frequency of riots staged by Muslim hooligans. And the British are no more there to take the blame except for those morons who will continue to explain in terms of British machinations everything that goes wrong in India till the end of time.

IT IS ISLAM THAT SEPARATES THE MUSLIMS FROM THE HINDUS

The Muslims in India are, by and large, the same people as the Hindus, except for a microscopic minority which takes pride in its descent from foreign forefathers. The Muslims in India share a lot with the Hindus in such externalia as race, language, dress, mores and manners. What is it, then, which divides the Muslims from the Hindus and sets them as a people apart? A correct answer to this question will go a long way in putting the problem in its proper perspective.

The answer is obvious as well as inescapable, unless we fall victim to the Marxist metaphysics according to which the Hindus are the haves and the Muslims the have-nots, and the conflict between the two is a disguised form of class conflict. There should be no doubt that it is Islam which divides the Muslims from the Hindus. Hindus would have to understand Islam if they want to understand Muslim Separatism, and thus rise to the challenge with an adequate response.

THE ESSENCE OF ISLAM

We give below the conclusions which cannot be avoided if we study the corpus of Islam from its original sources — the Quran, the Hadis, the biographies of the Prophet, and the compendia from the four leading schools of Islamic law — without getting caught in the casuistries which 19th and 20th century Islamic apologetics has woven round this creed:

1. The *Kalima* or the confession of faith (*īmān*) in Islam proclaims that there is no god except Allah, and that Muhammad is *the* Prophet (*rasūl*) of Allah. Which means that all Hindu Gods and Goddesses are non-existent or false, and that all Hindu sages and saints (*rishis* and *munis*) whether born before or after Muhammad was made *the* Prophet by Allah, are impostors or have been superseded.
2. Allah says that the Quran is the last as well as the best revelation which has superseded all earlier revelations of divine truth, and ruled out any future revelation till the end of time. Which means that all Hindu guides to spiritual seeking (*Śruti*) have become null and void, and that Hindus who continue to look up to them are no more than misguided fools.
3. Allah also says that he has perfected the code of human conduct in the life-style (*Sunnah*) of the Prophet, both for becoming virtuous in this life and for entering paradise hereafter. Which means that all Hindu codes of conduct (*Dharmaśāstras*) have become invalid, and can lead only to vice in this life and hell hereafter. Nor do Hindus have a right to evolve any code of conduct in future.
4. The Quran as well as the Sunnah informs us that the age preceding the prophethood of Muhammad was an age of ignorance (*jāhiliyyah*), and that all cultural creations of that age have either to be so converted as to fit into the framework of Islamic culture, or destroyed root and branch. Which means that the entire culture which Hindus have inherited from their hoary past has either to be forced into Islamic moulds or to be wiped out altogether.
5. Islam assures us that Allah has bestowed the whole world together with all its wealth and population upon his Chosen People, the congregation of Muhammad (*Ummat al-Muhammadī*), and that the lives, properties, and honour of the infidels (*kāfirs*) stands

> forfeited in favour of the believers (*mu'mins*). Which means that Hindus have become squatters in their ancestral homeland, and that Muslims have an unalienable right to drive them away, kill them, plunder them, enslave them, and dishonour them in every way till they agree to be converted to the only true faith.

In short, Islam divides the human family into two factions — the believers and the infidels—, human history into two periods — the age of ignorance and the age of enlightenment—, and the inhabited earth into two camps—, the lands of the believers (*Dār-ul-Islām*) and the lands of the infidels (*Dār-ul-harb*)—, and postulates a permanent war between these divisions. The believers are called upon to wage an unceasing war (*jihād*) on the infidels till the latter are converted or killed off. The age of enlightenment should strive in the same way till everything belonging to the age of ignorance is remoulded or replaced. And the *Dār-ul-Islām* should continue to send missions to the *Dār-ul-harb* till the latter is conquered and converted into *Dār-ul-Islām*.

One can well imagine the behaviour pattern of those who pass under the spell of Islam. They cannot but look upon their non-Muslim neighbours as enemies to be attacked on the slightest pretext, to be converted by all means, and to be eliminated if they (non-Muslims) prove intractable. *The Tragic Story of Partition* has given a detailed account of the behaviour pattern which started unfolding as soon as Islam bared its fangs during the Khilafat agitation. But being a typical Hindu who cannot help honouring Islam as a religion, the author has failed to trace the behaviour pattern back to the belief system.

Chapter XII
PLEA FOR A HISTORICAL PERSPECTIVE

Shri H.V. Seshadri has taken *The Tragic Story of Partition* to its fatal finale in 1947. Each of his chapters is packed with facts, insights, and interpretations such as make his book a substantial contribution to the large literature on this controversial subject. The only drawback in this otherwise well-documented study is the frequent absence of dates on which the books from which he has quoted were published, and the statements of leaders he has cited were made. Some of the statements credited to some national leaders leave the impression as if these leaders were able to see the precipice towards which our people were being pushed. Absence of dates on which these statements were made, helps in hiding the habit of our leaders to feel wise by hindsight.

We will not follow the trail of the tragedy farther than we have done. Our object in writing these review articles was to highlight the historical background against which this dismal drama was enacted in the last three decades preceding Partition. Congressmen in general and Communists in particular have joined hands with the residues of Islamic imperialism in propagating the Big Lie that Partition was provoked by 'Hindu communalism which was not prepared to concede even the minimum democratic demands of the Muslim minority', and which 'vitiated the atmosphere by wave after wave of Hindu revivalism'. On the other hand, the facts of recorded history tell an entirely different story. These facts lead only to one conclusion, namely, that the demand for Pakistan was not a sudden development precipitated by 'Hindu diehardism'. The seeds of that demand were always there in the Muslim psychology of separatism inspired by the ideology of Islam. What happened in the 'twenties, the 'thirties, and the 'forties was that those seeds sprouted rather fast in an environment made favourable by the confusion and the cowardice prevailing in the nationalist ranks.

THE BASIC AND THE BIG MISTAKE

The basic and the big mistake made by the national leadership was that it could not conceive of a native nationalism which would march ahead under its own impetus even if the Muslims were reluctant to participate in it or remained hostile to it. The national leadership was all along in a hurry to bargain with the British on the basis of Hindu-Muslim unity, and consequently failed to give sufficient thought and attention to the consolidation of genuine nationalist forces. The residues of Islamic imperialism spotted this weakness of the national leadership very soon, and exploited it to the hilt. Their price for co-operation went on soaring in direct proportion to the nationalist solicitation for it. The national leadership went on compromising the basic principles of nationalism till it landed itself in the trap of the Khilafat agitation. And the violence that followed that agitation frightened the national leadership out of its wits. After that, the Muslim League had only to threaten 'dire consequences' to make the national leadership shake in its skin, and appease 'the Muslim minority' at any cost.

The national leadership could have avoided this calamitous course by going to the sources of Muslim separatism and by identifying the spearheads of this separatism as residues of Islamic imperialism rather than as leaders of a bonafide minority. That needed a historical perspective which the national leadership either did not possess, or did not entertain when it was presented to it by the more perspective analysts of the situation. The need for a historical perspective is as great today as it was at that time because the same Muslim separatism is still rampant in the guise of new slogans, and the same residues of Islamic imperialism are rising again to stake their claims for unjust privileges and unequal power. Their ultimate aim is to restore the power of Islam in the India that has survived Partition. We will, therefore, end this series by providing the historical perspective as we see it so that the game of Islamic imperialism may be detected and defeated before it is too late.

THE FOREIGN FRATERNITY

Wave after wave of Muslims from Islamized lands abroad had poured into India for several centuries in the wake of Islamic invasions. They were the swordsmen, missionaries, and minions of Islamic imperialism. Most of them had forced Hindu women into matrimony or concubinage and fathered a prolific progeny on them. Some of them had also taken to Hindu mores and manners to a certain extent, particularly in matters of song and dance and other modes of entertainment. But in spite of everything, they had remained a foreign fraternity in forcible occupation of a land which did not belong to them except by right of conquest, and which they never loved as their motherland. They had continued to despise and lord it over not only their Hindu subjects but also the native converts whom they had forced or lured into the fold of Islam. In fact, their contempt for the native converts was deeper than that for their Hindu subjects. They had all along looked down upon the native converts as *Ajlāf* (low-born) and *Arzāl* (base-born) as compared to the *Ashrāf* (exalted) which distinctive designation they had reserved for themselves.

Muslim rule in India was never a process of continuous expansion and consolidation. It broke down again and again, and was re-established every time by a fresh wave of Islamic invaders from abroad. But it fell down finally and completely in the first half of the 18th century, and could not be salvaged even by the invasions of Ahmad Shah Abdali whom the *Ashrāf* had invited for putting down forces of national resurgence. Almost all parts of the country which had once been under Muslim rule passed under the sway of this or that Hindu power. The provincial Muslim dynasties like those at Lucknow and Hyderabad could save themselves from extinction only by entering into a subordinate alliance with the rising power of British imperialism. It was the power of British bayonets and not its own intrinsic strength which had preserved the privileged position of an alien Muslim minority in several parts of the country.

The Vijayanagara Empire had effectively prevented the percolation of a privileged Muslim class in large parts of South India. The Rajputs had never permitted this class to plant itself in Rajasthan, Bundelkhand, and Baghelkhand. Later on, the Marathas had taken care of this class in Maharashtra, Gujarat, Central India, and Orissa. The Sikhs had done the same in the Punjab, Kashmir, and the North-West Frontier Province. The Jats had taken care of it around its imperial seats at Agra and Delhi. Assam had all along remained out of its reach. It would have met the same fate in U.P., Bihar, Bengal, and the territories ruled by the Nizam but for the British intervention which gave it a new lease of life. It was in these provinces that the residues of Islamic imperialism regrouped themselves for a renewed bid not only for retaining their unjust privileges, but also for restoring Muslim power in the rest of India in course of time.

HINDUS COULD HAVE WIPED OUT ISLAM

It is to be noted that the Hindu powers that had risen on the ruins of Muslim rule, had nowhere behaved like the Islamic barbarians of yester years. Hindu princes could have easily done away with the descendants of foreign adventurers as the latter's forefathers had done earlier in the case of Hindu ruling classes. They could have easily brought back the native converts to the fold of the latter's ancestral religion and culture. They could have also reclaimed and restored to their original architecture and use the thousands of mosques, *mazārs*, *khānqahs* and palaces which had been built over the sites and, many a time, with the debris of demolished *mandirs*, monasteries, and other Hindu monuments.

That Hindu princes never did any of these things and that many of them gave employment to Muslim mercenaries in all positions, high and low, may go to their credit or discredit according to differing perceptions. But what cannot be gainsaid is that the residues of Islamic imperialism had no valid cause for complaint if Islam had been an alternate way of worship. The subsequent behaviour of the residues of Islamic imperialism in areas subdued by Indian nationalism, however, gave ample proof that, far from being an alternate way of worship, Islam was an imperialist ideology dressed up in religious verbiage. This was proved conclusively when the residues of Islamic imperialism in U.P., Bihar, and Bengal raised a hue and cry in defence of their unequal privileges, and their kinsmen elsewhere joined them with unconcealed enthusiasm.

RESIDUES OF ISLAMIC IMPERIALISM IN DIFFERENT ROLES

To start with, the residues of Islamic imperialism, led by Sir Syed Ahmed Khan in U.P. and Ameer Ali in Bengal, were very fond of stressing that they were a 'race of conquerors' who had enjoyed a 'monopoly of power and wealth only a hundred years ago'. Their appeal to the British government was to recognize the 'political importance' of their class. The British response was positive for quite some time. The British imperialists were getting worried over the rising tide of Indian nationalism. Thus the residues of Islamic imperialism became parasitic upon British imperialism, and strengthened their position by gaining the Partition of Bengal and separate electorates.

But there was a limit beyond which even the British could not go in their game of patronising Muslim separatism. They had not only to keep in mind the power of Indian nationalism which had reached a high stage in the Swadeshi Movement, and the spread of revolutionary activities in several parts of the country. They had also to yield to Indian nationalism in the matter of languages of administration at the lower levels, and in recruitment to public services by competitive examinations. This was what the residues of Islamic imperialism found absolutely intolerable. The situation was further complicated by the involvement of Britain in some foreign policy moves which ran counter to the Pan-Islamic pre-occupations of the residues of Islamic imperialism. For a while, the 'race of conquerors' found itself in a difficult predicament. The national movement was forging ahead in spite of their hostility to it. The British were finding it difficult to meet more of their demands at home and abroad.

It was at this critical juncture that the frustrated fraternity of foreign Muslims took a very strategic step. They started swearing by a solidarity with the native Muslims whom they had despised so far. They let loose on the native Muslims an army of mercenary Mullahs recruited, mostly from their own ranks. These Mullahs went about broadcasting the message that 'Islam was in danger', and that 'Hindus were out to enslave and exploit the Muslim minority'. It was in this manner that the residues of Islamic imperialism managed to 'merge' themselves with the native converts, and to present themselves at the head of a strong phalanx pitted against whatever historical forces threatened their unjust privileges. Hitherto, the haughty *Ashrāf* had stood strictly aloof from the abject *Ajlāf* and the despised *Arzāl*. Now all of a sudden the latter became the former's 'brothers in faith'. This was a tremendous transformation of the political scene in the second decade of the 20th century.

And to top it all, the residues of Islamic imperialism started referring to themselves as 'simple and straightforward fellows' as compared to the Hindus whom they named as the 'wily *baniās*'. The rogues' gallery played this act again and again, and succeeded in producing a dramatic effect, not only among the Muslim masses but also among the English-educated Hindu elite. The act was perfected over a period of time and played before larger and larger audiences with the help of an illiterate press controlled mostly by Hindu moneybags. A motley crowd of self-alienated but self-righteous Hindu politicians and scribes came forward to provide the applause. There was one note that became the refrain in the melancholy music which accompanied the act. The refrain that raised its pitch with the passing of every day, was that the Muslims had been deprived of an empire by the wily British, that the same British had suppressed and oppressed the Muslims in the aftermath of 1857, that the Muslims had been driven to become educationally backward and economically depressed in successive periods, and that the Hindu moneylenders in the countryside and the Hindu capitalists in the urban centres had been exploiting the Muslim peasants and workers.

The British were not impressed by this demonstration of 'Muslim power', or presentation of 'Muslim poverty'. They went ahead with the annulment of the Partition of Bengal, and enlargement of competitive examinations for recruitment to public services. The Montague-Chemsford Report expressed serious doubts about the very concept of separate electorates. In the international arena, too, the British supported the dismemberment of Turkey. They knew it very well that though the residues of Islamic imperialism could produce a lot of sound and fury and also become a law and order problem in several parts of the country, they were incapable of mobilizing the nation as a whole. The British never attached more than a nuisance value to this noisy fraternity which had to be befriended or ignored according to the needs of British policy at any time.

It was the national leadership which was impressed by this mobilisation of the 'Muslim masses' and the pathos of 'Muslim plight'. They accepted not only separate electorates but also weightages for the 'Muslim minority' in many provinces. They thought that they were beating the British at the latter's own game. The cries of 'Hindu-Muslim Bhāi Bhāi' raised by Muslim mobs in the aftermath of the Lucknow Pact and during the Khilafat agitation, blinded them to the game which the residues of Islamic imperialism were playing. They gladly offered their backs for carrying the dead-weight of Pan-Islamism. The residues of Islamic imperialism, who had been parasitic on British imperialism so far, now started to feed and fatten upon Indian nationalism. All this fanned the flames of Islamic fanaticism. It also gave birth to a brand of negative nationalism whose only stock-in-trade was anti-British hysteria. The die was thus cast, and what followed in subsequent years was a mere unfoldment of the drama which had already been scripted by Lokamanya Tilak, Mahatma Gandhi, and C.R. Das in all its salient features.

THE TRAGEDY OF NATIONAL LEADERSHIP

In the event, the national leadership repeated the story of the proverbial convict whom the judge had sentenced either to eat a hundred onions or to take a hundred shoe-strokes. The convict started by eating onions which soon made him sick with tearful eyes and a flowing nose. Next he chose to be beaten by shoes which exercise also produced very soon an unbearable pain in his body. Thereafter, he alternated between eating onions and suffering shoe-strokes, till he had eaten a hundred onions and received a hundred shoe-strokes. In like manner, the national leadership alternated between resisting and conceding Muslim demands which went on increasing. Resistance led to street riots which made the leadership panicky. Concessions led to more demands which forced the leadership to have second thoughts. Finally, the leadership conceded Partition in order to avoid bloodshed. But it ended by having Partition as well as a large-scale bloodshed in which millions were killed, maimed, ruined, and rendered homeless. The bloodshed would have certainly been on a smaller scale if the national leadership had opted for a civil war in the face of Muslim intransigence. It is doubtful if the residues of Islamic imperialism were in a position to pick up the gauntlet without British help which was no more available.

VOICES OF WARNING

Sri Aurobindo was the earliest to see a disastrous degeneration of national psychology, and sound a warning. Although he had retired from active politics several years earlier, his political perceptions had remained as sharp as ever. Speaking to a disciple on 18 April 1923, he had observed: "I am sorry they have made a fetish of Hindu-Muslim unity. *It is no use ignoring facts; some day the Hindus may have to fight the Muslims and they must prepare for it.* Hindu-Muslim unity should not mean the subjection of Hindus. Every time the mildness of the Hindu has given way. The best solution would be to allow the Hindus to organize themselves and Hindu-Muslim unity will take care of itself; it would automatically solve the problem. Otherwise, we are lulled into a false sense of satisfaction that we have solved the problem when in fact we have only shelved it."[1]

A few months later, on 13 July 1923, a disciple had observed that "There is also the question of Hindu-Muslim unity which the non-violence school is trying to solve on the basis of their theory". Sri Aurobindo had replied: "You can live amicably with a religion whose principle is toleration. But how is it possible to live with a religion whose principle is 'I will not tolerate?' How are you going to have unity with these people? Certainly Hindu-Muslim unity cannot be arrived at on the basis that Muslims will go on converting Hindus while Hindus shall not convert Mohammedans. You can't build unity on such basis. *Perhaps the only way of making the Mohammedans harmless is to make them lose their faith in their religion.*"[2]

Sri Seshadri has cited the advice which Sarat Chandra Chatterjee had tendered to his people. He had written as follows in October, 1926: "*Hindustan is the land of the Hindus.* It is, therefore, the duty of the Hindus alone to liberate it from the shackles of foreign domination. *Muslims are sitting with their faces turned towards Arabia or Turkey.* Their heart is not in the land of Hindustan. But when it is not there, it is no use lamenting over it. We need not be unnerved by counting the heads of Muslims. Numbers are not the supreme truth in the world... In freedom's battle in any country, do all the people of that country take part? When the Americans fought for their freedom, more than half the people of that country were with the British. In the Irish freedom

---

[1] *Evening Talks with Sri Aurobindo* recorded by A.B. Purani, Second Series, Pondicherry, 1974, p. 48. Emphasis added.

[2] Ibid, p. 50. Emphasis added.

struggle, how many were actually involved in it?... Right or wrong is not decided by the counting of heads. It is decided by the intensity of *tapasya* or the single-minded devotion to the cause. *The problem before the Hindus is not to devise ways and means of bringing about an artificial unity. The problem before them in how to organise themselves.*"[3]

Later on, the same line of Hindu consolidation was advocated by the Rashtriya Swayamsewak Sangh. The Hindu Mahasabha under the leadership of Veer Savarkar gave the clarion call to Hinduize politics and militarize the Hindus. It was the only right response to the grave situation created by a series of surrenders made by the national leadership in the face of the Muslim League goondaism. But the national leadership not only ignored these seers, sages, statesmen, and patriots of unimpeachable integrity; it also branded them as 'Hindu communalists'. That was a great sin. On the other hand, the same national leadership hugged to its bosom as 'nationalist Muslims' not only Islamic imperialists like Abdul Bari and Abul Kalam Azad but also Pan-Islamic conspirators and habitual embezzlers of public funds like the Ali Brothers. That was an unpardonable folly. The sin and the folly combined in due course to close every other option of the national leadership, and forced it into an abject surrender — acceptance of Partition.

SECULARISM: THE NEW SMOKE-SCREEN

The same sin and folly which the national leadership committed in the name of Hindu-Muslim unity in the years before Partition continue to be committed by *all* national political parties in the name of Secularism. Earlier, the residues of Islamic imperialism had acquired a veto on what could be called national; now they have acquired a veto on what could be called secular. Things have reached such a pass that no cause, no platform, no organization, and no political party can claim to be secular unless the residues of Islamic imperialism approve of it. Conversely, all causes, platforms, organizations, and political parties which do not countenance the claims of Islamic imperialism stand automatically condemned as 'Hindu communalist'. This is the conditioned reflex which seems to have been planted permanently in the national psyche.

And the rogues' gallery continues to play the same old act to which some more scenes have been added. The refrain now is that the 'Muslim minority' has not received its 'fair share' in the fruits of national development after the dawn of national independence, that the Muslims

[3] *The Tragic Story of Partition*, p. 252. Emphasis added.

remain a 'deprived and beleaguered minority' inside democratic India, that the 'life, property and honour' of Muslims are in constant danger from 'Hindu chauvinism', and that a secular state in which the 'Muslim minority is thus discriminated against and oppressed and threatened with genocide is a sham and a shame'. The line-up of grievances is so long and seems so impressive that even the most sceptical gets deceived. In any case, it provides good copy for Hindu scribes and scholars who spend most of their time in coffee shops but who nevertheless write so authoritatively on the socio-economic scene as if they had freshly arrived from a painstaking field study. And they also denounce as a 'Hindu communalist' any one who questions their credentials vis-a-vis this serious subject.

THE ONLY WAY OUT: AN AWAKENED HINDU SOCIETY

Hindu society by and large has become a poor society as a result of centuries of exploitation by Islamic and British imperialism. Unlike the Muslims and Christians in India, Hindu society has no patrons and financiers abroad and has to depend entirely on its own resources from inside its only homeland. The class which came to power on the strength of sacrifices made by Hindu society has turned its back on its benefactor, and continues to cultivate the sworn enemies of Hindu society in the name of Democracy and Secularism. Hindu society also suffers from a lack of leadership which can free it from the stranglehold of power-hungry politicians who divide it into smaller and smaller segments pitted against each other. Hindu-baiting has become a profitable profession for all sorts of penpushers. As a cumulative effect, Hindu society has lost its self-confidence, and has been thrown on the defensive by a variety of bullies and blackmailers. Such a society is in no shape to face the inroads of Islamic imperialism which remains as vicious today as it was in the years before Partition.

The first task before Hindu society is to recover its self-confidence. That can happen only if Hindu society re-awakens to its inimitable heritage — spiritual, cultural, and scientific — and stops treating totalitarian ideologies like Islam as anything other than falsehoods fattened by force and fraud. The rest will follow. A self-confident Hindu society will make a start by attaining the pride of place in its present-day homeland. It will assert itself as the nation rather than be treated condescendingly as one of several communities, or even as the majority community. Next, it will recover those parts of its ancestral homeland which have been lost to its enemies, as also those of its children who have been alienated from it in the past. Finally, it will hold its head high as the inheritor of a vast spiritual and cultural vision. A self-confident Hindu society alone can make its characteristic contributions to the present-day human society which is caught in the throes of an unprecedented spiritual and moral crisis.

APPENDIX
ISLAMIC MANIFESTO FOR INDIA

It is old. It is new. It is an enduring theme on which the Ulama and the Sufis of Islam thrive.

It is a rueful review of an opportunity lost in the past. It is a fond dream about a future fulfilment. It is a fanatic faith to fight for in the present.

Borrowing a metaphor from the *Communist Manifesto* of Karl Marx, the theme can be summarised as well as sloganized as follows: "We, the Ulama and the Sufis of Islam, disdain to hide our aim. We stand for a full and final conquest of India by Islam. Muslims of India unite! You have nothing to lose but your minority complex. You have a whole subcontinent to gain!"

The Ulama and the Sufis grieve that Islam was a failure in India in the final round, though it monopolised military as well as political power for five centuries and more. They envy the history of Islamic imperialism in Syria, Palestine, Persia, Central Asia, North Africa, Malaysia, and Indonesia where it succeeded in a total subversion of older societies and cultures in a far shorter span of time.

The Ulama and the Sufis hope and pray that Allah will be more merciful towards his favourite faith in the future, and enable them to establish a *hukumat-i-ilāhiyā* in India. They feel confident that this time they will not fail, and that they will use the opportunity fully for eradicating the last vestiges of *jāhiliyya* from this land.

The Ulama and the Sufis leave no stone unturned to keep their flock free from every 'taint' of empiricism, rationalism, universalism, and humanism. They also go in search of fresh pastures among the weaker sections of Hindu society. The name of the game is mass conversions to Islam.

In medieval times, when Islam ruled the roost, the most 'upright' Ulama and the 'saintliest' Sufis carried on a long-drawn-out debate regarding the treatment to be meted out to the Hindus conquered by the sword of Islam. They quoted chapter and verse from the Quran, the Hadis and the 'learned' commentaries to prove a proposition. The syllogism had more than the three standard steps. But the argument, they thought, was unassailable. The inexorable logic unfolded as follows:

1. The five categories of 'unbelievers' whom the Prophet came to know in his own lifetime were the Polytheists of Arabia, the Jews, the Christians, the Zoroastrians, and the Sabaeans;
2. The Prophet had no qualms about the Polytheists; they were to be

slaughtered unless they surrendered and became Muslims;

3. The Jews, the Christians and, later on, the Zoroastrians and the Sabaeans were recognized by the Prophet as *Ahl-i-Kitāb* (People of the Book);
4. The Prophet honoured them with the designation of *Zimmīs* who could be allowed to live in an Islamic state, provided they renounced resistance, and agreed to pay *jizyah*;
5. Umar, the second pious *Khalīfah* of Islam, spelled out in so many words the numerous disabilities to be imposed on the *Zimmīs*, reducing them to a status of non-citizens inside an Islamic state;
6. The Prophet had not known any Hindus in his own life-time and could not, therefore, receive a Revelation regarding their status in an Islamic state;
7. The Hindus were not *Ahl-i-Kitāb*; on the contrary, they were unashamed and outright Polytheists;
8. The Hindus, therefore, could not be designated as *Zimmīs* entitled to pay *jizyah* and live under disabilities imposed by an Islamic state;
9. The Islamic state in India was under an inescapable obligation to use all its power and resources to force the Hindus to embrace Islam, failing which they were to be sent to hell where they rightly belonged.

Quod erat demonstrandum. It was difficult to find a flaw in this logic without putting Islamic jurisprudence in jeopardy.

One could have, of course, faulted the syllogism by asking a simple question: "What happened to the Zoroastrians whom your Prophet had 'honoured' as *Zimmīs*? Did Islam allow them to live as *Zimmīs* in the beloved land of their birth? Where are they now?" But the Ulama and the Sufis of Islam have never acquired the 'bad habit' of asking or answering questions. They have always found it far more convenient to call for a cutting off of *kāfir* heads.

This, then, was the imperative of Islamic theology vis-a-vis the Hindus. But there were other realities such as the balance of power between the Islamic state and the Hindu society. In large parts of India, Hindus were far from being conquered completely. If pressed too hard, Hindus revolted, and imperilled the Islamic 'empire' itself. Hindus were also needed by the Islamic state as hewers of wood and drawers of water so that Muslim swordsmen, Ulama and Sufis, who had become the aristocracy, could enjoy the lands and the loot which Allah and his Prophet had bestowed upon them.

Some Sultans strived hard to carry out the commands of the Ulama and the Sufis. But they discovered very soon and to their great discomfiture that Hindus despised Islam as a species of barbarism, and fought back fiercely when driven to the wall. The Sultans had to admit defeat and die unfulfilled. Many Sultans of the imperial and provincial dynasties suffered this supreme frustration while attempting to forge ahead in the way of Allah.

The Hanafi school of Islamic 'law' came to the rescue of the Sultans who had found themselves between the devil of the Ulama and the Sufis, and the deep sea of Hindu resistance. This school searched the scriptures of Islam to find support for their contention that Hindus also could be designated as *Zimmīs,* and thus allowed to live in an Islamic state. So the Sultans indulged occasionally in the luxury of forced conversions, and killing of Hindus *en masse*. But, for the rest, they were content to collect *jizyah* and other back-breaking taxes from Hindus and enjoy in peace their imperial power and privilege, including harems crowded with Hindu women captured in war and otherwise.

A notable exception to these two types of Sultans was Akbar. He saw through the exclusive claims of Islam and kept the Ulama and the Sufis at an arm's length. He was favourably impressed by Hindu saints, sages, scholars and statesmen and became increasingly attached to them. He evolved a policy of *sulah-i-kul* between the Islamic state and the Hindu society. He abolished *jizyah*, banned cow-slaughter, permitted questions regarding the character of Islam and its Prophet, allowed Hindu converts to go back to their ancestral religion, and prohibited killing of Hindus for marrying Muslim women without getting converted to Islam. In short, he restored self-respect to the Hindus who came forward to help him in building a splendid and stable empire which came to be envied by the rest of the world.

But there is a strong element of atavism in Islam which prevents it from learning any lesson from history. Akbar's policy of peace came in for an adverse review in the reign of Shah Jahan and underwent a total reversal under Aurangzeb. This great *ghazi* of Islam declared a new *jihād* against the Hindus. The result was the ruin of the Mughal empire which crumbled within two decades after his death. Power now passed into the hands of Hindus—the Rajputs, the Marathas, the Jats and the Sikhs.

Islam is also famous for breeding a brand of fanatics who refuse to recognize objective reality and who love to live in a world of fantasy. The Ulama and the Sufis refused to believe that the imperial power of Islam in India was gone for good. Soon after the break-up of the Mughal empire, there arose Shah Waliullah (1702-1762) followed by his son, Abdul Aziz, followed by the latter's disciple, Syed Ahmad Barelvi (1786-1831), all of whom were possessed by the passionate idea — which they preached with great fervour — that the imperial power of Islam could and should be restored in India.

These early Don Quixotes of Islam were followed by others like Shariatullah (1790-1831), Dudhu Mian (1819-60), Titu Mian (1782-1831) and the Wahabis who titled their swords at the British power in Bengal and the Sikh sovereignty in the Punjab. They declared that India had once again become a *Dār-ul-harb* (enemy territory), and invited their brethren in faith to practise *jihād* or *hijrat*. They met the fate which such lunatics deserve, and disappeared into the dustbin of history. Only the Ulama and the Sufis hail them as *shahīds* (martyrs).

A new type of wisdom, though within the four walls of Islamic fanaticism and day-dreaming, dawned upon Khwaja Hasan Nizami in the early years of the 20th century. He was no ordinary pen-pusher or paid mullah in some suburban mosque. On the contrary, he was a highly placed 'divine' in the hierarchy of Nizamuddin Auliya's prestigious *silsilā,* and widely honoured in the Muslim world. He published in 1920 a big book, *Fātami Dāwat-i-Islam*, in which he advocated all means, fair and foul, by which Hindus were to be converted to Islam. He advised the mullahs to concentrate on Hindu 'untouchables', and convert them *en masse* so that Muslims could achieve parity of population with the Hindus. He disclosed in the introduction to his book that he had consulted many Muslim leaders including the Agha Khan regarding the soundness of his scheme, and that all of them had agreed with the caution that the scheme should be kept a closely guarded secret. Unfortunately for the Khwaja, the scheme came to the notice of Swami Shraddhananda who exposed it, fought it tooth and nail, and frustrated it completely by means of his Shuddhi Movement.

And now we have the same scheme resurrected before us by the Islamic Centre in London, in a still more ambitious form. The aim of achieving parity with the Hindus has been abandoned in favour of full Islamisation of India. The Islamic fraternity in India has welcomed the scheme with open arms. Jama't-i-Islami is the most fanatic constituent of this fraternity. There are many more individuals and organizations operating under different disguises. In any case, the scheme is being pushed ahead vigorously with the aid of petro-dollars. Many Islamic countries, particularly Kuwait, Libya, and Saudi Arabia, are its 'pious' patrons.

The full contours of this conspiracy were reveled by Javed Ansari in the December 1981 number of *Arabia*: *The Islamic Review* published by the Islamic Press Agency, London. The Agency is an expensive outfit maintained and financed by Saudi Arabia. Javed violated no oath of secrecy because the conspiracy became widely known in India as soon as it was hatched by a conference of Islamic embassies in the West. He only presented it in a finished form and with full self-confidence, so that no one was left in any doubt about its ramifications.

The article by Javed is titled *India: The World's 'Largest Democracy'*. We need not quarrel with his oblique reference to democracy in India. The 'gentleman' has in mind the Islamic 'democracies' of Pakistan, Iran, Libya, Saudi Arabia, Syria and the United Arab Emirates. What he writes in his article is much more interesting. The main point made by him comes at the end of the article. He says: "Such a programme would require first of all an abandonment of the strategy which gives priority to protecting the 'special status' and 'minority rights' of the Muslim community. No minority community can have such 'rights' within the existing Indian system. The only realistic political option is to develop an alternative vision of India's future — a vision capable of mobilising all sections of the Indian people into making sacrifice for its realisation."

What is the alternative vision? Javed does not mince words. His clarion call is loud and clear. He announces: "Islam must be presented as an ideological framework capable of redefining the social perspective of the ordinary Indian citizen. Islam must emerge as a cohesive social force challenging the hegemony of both nationalism and socialism in India. This is a difficult and challenging task, calling for the building of a new political and social base."

Who is going to provide that political and social base? Javed concludes: "The movement of the Harijans towards Islam provides a rare opportunity of initiating this struggle. If this opportunity is missed, India's Muslims will have lost a chance to play a decisive role in the making of history."

We have suspected for a long time that Islam is not a religion as the protagonists of *sarva-dharma-samabhāva* would have us believe. We are, therefore, grateful to Javed for conceding that Islam is an ideology. A discussion about the nature of that ideology need not deter us here. At the moment we are concerned with the way that ideology is being presented by the spokesmen of Islam.

It is not an accident that over the past several years the emphasis has suddenly shifted from the 'scriptures' to the 'social message' of Islam. Islam is still being presented as the 'only true religion'. But a louder noise is being made about Islamic society being an ideal society.

There is an implied admission that the 'scriptures' of Islam have failed it in India over the long stretch of some 1300 years. So the 'social philosophy of Islam' is being given a turn to try its luck in the same old game of subversion.

Again, we do not want to be detained by discussion about the nature of Islamic 'social philosophy'. That discussion will be taken up in due course. Here we are concerned with how that 'philosophy' is being presented to us at this time.

Islam, we are told, stands for the Brotherhood of Man and an equalitarian social order free from caste hierarchy, class oppression, economic exploitation, and so on. It all sounds as if Islam is another version of Communism . Haven't we been told by some noted spokesman that Communism is Islam minus Allah, or that Allah plus Communism constitutes Islam? But we shall not press home the parallel.

What is the social milieu in which this 'ideal' social order has to operate? Well, it is the goddammed Hindu society "encumbered with gross inequality, economic exploitation, caste cruelties, oppression of women", and so on. The 'ideal' social order has to overcome and destroy this wicked social order and "redeem" these 700 million human beings from fate "worse than that of the beasts and worms". The logic is irrefutable, however irritating it may be to "our brethren of the Hindu fold".

There was a time when the spokesmen of Islam stood alone in performing the painful task of telling the truth about the Hindu social order. Recently they have been relieved of that burden by a large tribe of Hindu scribes and scholars serving in the daily and the periodical press owned by Hindu moneybags. They have dragged out no end of skeletons hidden in the Hindu cupboard. They have left us in no doubt about the enormous inequalities handed down by the hoary Hindu heritage. Damn Hinduism and get publicity as a secularist and a progressive! That is the bait held out by some notable editors. Many scribes rise to the bait because the payment they receive is much better. Many politicians swallow the bait — hook, line and sinker — simply because a periodical enjoys a large circulation. No politician worth his salt can ignore publicity in the prestigious press.

It is not an accident that in recent years we have been flooded with news about 'atrocities on Harijans'. A selective news-reporting in the press leaves the unmistakable impression that Harijans are the only people who are being beaten up, burnt, and killed otherwise in our countryside; that Harijan women are the only women being molested by 'caste' Hindus; and that Harijan labourers are the only labourers getting buried under the debris of defective constructions. The reporters who collect these stories and the editors who display them on the front page have a glow of self-righteous satisfaction on their faces. It is never news for them that Brahmins, Thakurs and other 'caste' Hindus also get killed in similar fracas; that 'caste' Hindu girls also get molested and forced into prostitution; and that non-Harijan Hindu labourers also get buried in like manner. The same Hindu scribes and scholars have started singing the glories of the Islamic Brotherhood of Man.

It is this spectacle of breast-beating on the part of the Hindu elite which has emboldened the spokesmen of Islam to rewrite India's history vis-a-vis the swordsmen of Islamic imperialism. According to Javed, "Islam came to India at the invitation of the peasants of Sindh who were the victims of colonial central Indian rule in the 7th century. Muhammad bin Qasim, the liberator of Sind, was immensely popular among the mases."

Several Muslim historians of Sindh tell us in so many words that Sindh had been an independent kingdom for more than 150 years at the time it was invaded by the Arab armies. Al-Biladhuri writes in *Futūh-ul-Buldān* that between 659 and 712 A.D, five Arab expeditions were defeated and dispersed, and their commanders killed at the borders of Sindh by the Jats and the Meds before Muhammad bin Qasim succeeded in his mission of murder, rapine and loot. Does it all look like a guest party of Muslims who the peasants of Sindh were waiting for in order to extend a warm welcome? The *Chuchnāmah* based on a contemporary Muslim account describes in detail how the Jat peasantry fought fiercely for every inch of the motherland, and how it died but did not surrender. Brazen faced liars like Javed will have to make a bonfire of many histories of Islam written by pious Muslims in medieval times before their concoctions can have a chance.

But while lying about Hindus and their history, Javed has told the truth about the Sufis. He writes: "It was the sufi saints who initiated the struggle for the establishment of an Islamic state in India. Khwaja Muinuddin Chisti, Khwaja Nizamuddin Aulia and Bakhtiyar Kaki opposed the secularist policies of the kings of the slave dynasty of medieval India. Mujadid al-Thani Ahmed Sirhindi organized a resistance movement against the Mughal Emperor Akbar and his attempts to establish a secular Indian polity. The Mujidid's disciples and devotees included Akbar's great-grandson, the dervish Prince Aurangzeb Alamgeer."

It is an interesting disclosure about the Sufis. Many Hindus who have no illusions about prophetic Islam have a very soft corner for the

Sufis whom Islam has been presenting as its saints for the past so many years. But the painful truth is that the 'Mystic Dimension of Islam' has always been the ideological arsenal of Islamic imperialism.

Javed has also informed us about the newly acquired self-confidence of Islam in India. He proclaims: "The Muslims of India are more committed to Islamic ideology, better politically organized and exhibit greater unity to-day than at any time since independence. It is this new-found sense of destiny which has enabled them to welcome the Harijans into Islam throughout India and to assert their right to formulate a national, social and political strategy which is distinct and uniquely Islamic...This community is rapidly adopting the view that their destiny in inextricably linked to that of India. India must undergo a social and a political transformation before the bulk of its population can escape from social deprivation and exploitation."

This self-confidence is symbolised by the waxing fortunes of Jama't-i-Islami, the vanguard of the Islamic crusade in this country. Javed reports: "This view has been consistently expounded by the Jamaat Islami since 1947 when it was an insignificant political grouping with little or no influence. It numbered its supporters in hundreds and its message of preaching Islam 'daawa' and downgrading the importance of 'minority interests' evoked almost no response. However, the Jamaat-i-Islami Annual Convention held in Hyderabad last July attracted more than 10,000 participants. Its literature has now been translated into 17 Indian languages. Thousands of Hindus count themselves amongst its supporters."

That brings us to the beginning. We have to give a vote of thanks to Javed. He starts his article by the following statement: "Since 1947, India, a leading champion of secularism and the home of the most ancient philosophies known to man has witnessed more than 20,000 incidents of serious communal rioting. Every year the number of Muslims who fall victim grows larger." We leave the statistics in this statement to the Government of India. They have been cited by a spokesman of the Arabs whose causes our Government defends, day in and day out. But we cannot help being grateful to Javed for presenting India as the "home of the most ancient philosophies known to man". We do not mind it at all that the compliment carries as a taunt. Truth needs telling, whatever the twist. The worst liar in the world has a right to tell the truth once in a while.

We wish and hope that the Ulama and the Sufis of Islam in Indian will also admit this great truth, and stop denouncing this country as an area of darkness which 'Islam has to illumine'. We appeal to the worthies of the Jama't-i-Islami in particular and Muslims in general to study some of these "most ancient philosophies" to which Javed has referred. We assure them that they will find it a refreshing change from the cock-and-bull stories on which they have been fed so far by the Quran and the Hadis.

INDEX